CESSATIONISM
or
CONTINUATIONISM?

An Exposition Of 1 Corinthians 12-14
And Related Passages

About the author

Boon-Sing Poh was born in Malaysia in 1954. Brought up in a pagan background, he was saved by God's grace through faith in Jesus Christ while studying in the United Kingdom. He returned to Malaysia to become a lecturer in a university for six years, founded the first Reformed Baptist Church in the country in 1983, and was imprisoned for his faith from 1987 to 1988 for a period of 325 days. He is the pastor of Damansara Reformed Baptist Church (DRBC) in Kuala Lumpur, a contented husband, a thankful father of four sons, and a happy grandfather. He earned the PhD degree in Electronics Engineering from the University of Liverpool, UK, the Diploma in Religious Study from Cambridge University, UK, and the PhD degree in Theology from North-West University, SA.

CESSATIONISM
or
CONTINUATIONISM?

An Exposition Of 1 Corinthians 12-14

And Related Passages

BOON-SING POH

Published by
Good News Enterprise

This book is dedicated to

Dr. Stuart Olyott

in acknowledgement of

all that I have learned,

under God, from him.

Contents

PREFACE TO THIS EDITION

A good half-a-century has passed since the Charismatic movement emerged, morphing from the earlier Pentecostal movement of the 1930's. The latter arose after the split among the "Fundamentalists" (or Old Evangelicals), following the Fundamentalist-Modernist Controversy, into three camps – viz. the (new) Fundamentalists, the Reformed, and the Neo-Evangelicals. Individuals from the four groups (including the Pentecostals) realigned themselves as they interacted – a process that continues to this day.

In the earlier years of the Charismatic movement, excesses such as dancing, falling to the ground upon being touched ('to be slain by the Spirit'), mooing like cows, and writhing on the ground like snakes were seen apart from claims of visions, prophecy, tongue-speaking and healings. While such excesses are seldom heard of today, claims of visions, prophecy, tongue-speaking and healings continue to be made. Those who hold to the continuation of such 'sign gifts' prefer to be known as Continuationists, eschewing the negative name of Non-Cessationists. Traditionally, the Evangelicals held to Cessationism. Today, many Neo-Evangelicals hold to Continuationism, while some Charismatics who have embraced Calvinistic soteriology are mistakenly calling themselves Reformed. There are individuals who were formerly of Reformed persuasion but have embraced Continuationism.

While we rejoice when others embrace the truths we hold dear to, it is a matter of regret that there are those who do not see the inconsistency of Reformed theology with Continuationism. There is still a need to put forward the biblical case for Cessationism. It is hoped that this book will contribute towards that end, thereby clarifying the issue for many and weaning others off Continuationism. This book remains substantially the same as its first edition, published under the title of "Tongues, Prophecy, Healings..."

Boon-Sing Poh,
Kuala Lumpur, April 2020.

PREFACE

There are many books which helpfully clarify the controversy over the charismatic gifts. Most of them have adopted a topical approach, in which Bible passages are expounded only as they have a bearing on the subject under consideration. Others have used arguments from the perspective of biblical theology, showing that the gifts should be understood in the context of the unfolding will of God in history. Some have assessed the gifts from a historical point of view.

This writer has for a long while perceived that a direct and systematic exposition of 1 Corinthians 12-14 will be helpful towards settling the faith of many on the subject. It will complement the other books already published on the subject. A commentary on the whole book of 1 Corinthians, while possessing merits of its own, will tend to distract from the immediate objective. What is needed is an exposition of the relevant chapters so that the claims of the Charismatic movement may be assessed in their light. This book is an attempt to fulfil this perceived need.

The substance of this book comes from a series of talks given at various places over the years. This accounts for its form and style. It is directed to the ordinary Christians, and not just to pastors and teachers. It is nevertheless meat, and not milk. Effort and concentration are needed to follow these studies. The reader who wishes to grow must be prepared to chew over God's word and digest the truths it yields.

Unless otherwise indicated, the Bible quotations are from the New King James version (copyright 1979, 1980, 1982) published by Thomas Nelson, Inc. Reference is made occasionally to Vine's Expository Dictionary of Old and New Testament Words (copyright 1981 by Fleming H. Revell Company), published by World Bible Publishers.

The author would like to express his sincere thanks to Ms. Yeo Kim Eng (now with the Lord), a retired school teacher, and Rev. Michael Harley, the pastor of West Woolwich Church, London, (now pastor of Friston Baptist Chapel, Suffolk) for their painstaking proof-reading of the manuscript.

Boon-Sing Poh,
Kuala Lumpur, 1997.

One

THE AUTHORITY OF SCRIPTURE
(2 Timothy 3:16-17)

Controversies abound in the churches. Some controversies are not worth engaging in, for they have to do with matters that are not important. Titus 3:9 says, "Avoid foolish disputes, genealogies, contentions, and strivings about the law; for they are unprofitable and useless." There are many occasions, however, when the faithful Christian must engage in controversies in order to defend the truth. He has "to contend earnestly for the faith which was once for all delivered to the saints" (Jude 3). Failure to contend for the faith is failure to be faithful to the Lord and to His word. Furthermore, retreat from controversial issues will not help our own faith, since we will then remain unsure of the issues that are the subject of controversy.

All controversies must be settled by the word of God. Scripture is our "ruler" or "standard of measure". To know the dimensions of, say, a table, we must have an agreed standard of measure. It will not do if I have a ruler which is not of the same length as yours when both of them are supposed to be one metre long. If we do not have an agreed source of authority, there will be no possibility of coming to an agreement about anything. Communications will breakdown. There will be no common ground for discussion. We must agree that Holy Scripture should be our only source of authority.

There are those who argue that we must be guided by the Holy Spirit rather than by Scripture. That sounds so pious and correct but in reality it is nothing other than pious talk. The Holy Spirit causes a person to be born again by the hearing of God's word. It says in Romans 10:17, "Faith *comes* by hearing, and hearing by the word of God." We are told in 1 Peter 1:23 that a person is "born again, not of corruptible seed but incorruptible, through the word of God which lives and abides forever". The Holy Spirit does not work without means. He uses the word of God to bring about the new birth.

That is not all. The Holy Spirit also uses the word of God to sanctify, guide and build up a believer. A believer must "grow in the grace and knowledge of our Lord and Saviour Jesus Christ" (2 Peter 3:18). We are told, in Romans 12:2, "Do not be conformed to this world, but be transformed by the renewing of your mind, that you may prove what is that good and acceptable and perfect will of God." We are told in Ephesians 5:26 that Jesus Christ is sanctifying the church "with the washing of water by the word".

To be guided by the Holy Scripture is to be guided by the Holy Spirit. It was the Holy Spirit who moved men to write the Scripture. We are told, in 2 Timothy 3:16-17, "All Scripture *is* given by inspiration of God, and *is* profitable for doctrine, for reproof, for correction, for instruction in righteousness, that the man of God may be complete, thoroughly equipped for every good work." Since all of Scripture is inspired by God, or "God-breathed", it possesses an authority that is unique. It reveals God, and His will, to us. If we wish to know the true God, and His will for men, we must turn to His word. Psalm 138:2 says, "You have magnified Your word above all Your name."

We must agree, then, that the Scripture should be the only authority in all matters of faith and practice. But what do we mean by this?

1.1 Scripture Is The Sole Authority

Complete
Firstly, this means that the revealed will of God as contained in
the Bible is complete. There is no more revelation to be added
to what is already there in the Scripture.

We must note that the "all Scripture" of 2 Timothy 3:16-17
is a reference to more than the Old Testament scriptures. It
includes also the New Testament.

The Old Testament scriptures are called "the Holy Scriptures", or "the sacred writings", in verse 15. There, Paul says
to Timothy, "...from childhood you have known the Holy Scriptures, which are able to make you wise for salvation through
faith which is in Christ Jesus." Timothy must continue in the
things learned, not only from the Old Testament scriptures,
but also from Paul himself (verses 10- 14; 1:13; 2:2). Paul and
all the other apostles were aware of the fact that they were
conveying God's word to the church. When Paul wrote to the
Thessalonian Christians, he said, "For this reason we also thank
God without ceasing, because when you received the word of
God which you heard from us, you welcomed it not as the word
of men, but as it is in truth, the word of God, which also effec-
tively works in you who believe" (1 Thessalonians 2:13). In 2
Peter 3:15-16, Peter says this of Paul's writings: "...our beloved
brother Paul, according to the wisdom given to him, has written to you, as also in all his epistles, speaking in them of these
things, in which are some things hard to understand, which
untaught and unstable *people* twist to their own destruction,
as *they do* also the rest of the Scriptures".

The apostles expected the revelation of God to be completed, so that the church will be established upon "the foundation of the apostles and prophets, Jesus Christ Himself being
the chief cornerstone" (Ephesians 2:20). When John wrote the
book of Revelation in AD 96, on the island of Patmos, he must
have known that, as the last surviving apostle, he was writing the final instalment of God's word. The well-known verses
found at the end the book of Revelation, although intended

to end that book, must be seen as covering the whole Bible as well: "For I testify to everyone who hears the words of the prophecy of this book: If anyone adds to these things, God will add to him the plagues that are written in this book; and if anyone takes away from the words of the book of this prophecy, God shall take away his part from the Book of Life, from the holy city, and *from* the things which are written in this book" (Revelation 22:18-19).

The warning is given in this passage that God will severely judge those who tamper with His word, either by taking away any part of it, or by adding to it. The same command was given in the Old Testament, in Deuteronomy 4:2 and 12:32, although not in the same fullness. God's word is given to be obeyed, not to be tampered with. The prophets of God wrote the Old Testament books, and the apostles and prophets of Christ wrote the New Testament books. The Old Testament scriptures pointed to the coming of Christ, and the New Testament books completed the teachings of the Christ who had come. The gospel is now completely revealed. This is "the mystery" referred to in the Bible (Ephesians 3:9; Colossians 1:24-29: Romans 16:25-26). This is the gospel age, "the last days", in which the elect are being called out of the world by the preaching of the gospel (Acts 2:17, 21; Matthew 28:20).

The Scripture is complete.

Sufficient
Secondly, when we say that Scripture is the sole authority, we mean that it is sufficient for all our needs. We are told in our text that Scripture is profitable for doctrine, for reproof, for correction, for instruction in righteousness....". Only four categories of "profits" or benefits are mentioned, but these cover all areas of our lives. We cannot find any area of life which is not covered by one or more of these categories – whether it is our job, marriage, the raising children, or whatever. These four categories – doctrine, reproof, correction, and instruction in righteousness – are all-encompassing.

Take for example the issue of watching the television. Are

we to watch the television? What sort of programmes may we watch? The television is not harmful in itself. The programmes we watch must be governed by such truths as are found in Philippians 4:8: "Whatever things *are* true, whatever things *are* noble, whatever things *are* just, whatever things *are* pure, whatever things *are* lovely, whatever things *are* of good report, if *there is* any virtue and if *there is* anything praiseworthy – meditate on these things."

Take another example. Is it right for a Christian to gamble? We answer, "No!", although there is no explicit statement in Scripture that a believer may not gamble. We are certain that a Christian may not gamble because it leads to covetousness, discontent with what one has, trust in "chance" instead of in God, and addiction to gambling. All these are contrary to the teachings of the Bible (Colossians 3:5; 1 Timothy 6:8; Matthew 6:33; 1 Corinthians 6:20; John 8:36). It also causes the person to seek riches by the easy way out instead of earning a living by hard and honest work (2 Thessalonians 3:10).

We see then, from these examples, that Scripture is sufficient for all our needs. It is sufficient for the man of God to "be complete, thoroughly equipped for every good work". Note what the text says: *complete, thoroughly equipped, for every good work.*

Final
Thirdly, when we say the Scripture is the sole authority we mean that it is *final*. This means that the teaching of the Bible must be accepted as correct; it must not be questioned; instead, we must submit ourselves to it. We are not saying that we accept whatever people teach us as the correct teaching of the Bible. We must "take heed how we hear" (Luke 8:18). We must weigh up what we hear. We must search the Scripture ourselves, like what the Bereans did, to find out whether the teaching is really correct (Acts 17:1-12). However, once the true teaching of Scripture is established, we must bow to it.

An illustration will help. In Malaysia, there are three levels in the legal system. In the first level, a person can be tried in the magistrate's court, the sessions court, or the high court, depending on the seriousness of the case. If he is dissatisfied with the verdict of the court, he may appeal to the next level, which is the Court of Appeal, for a hearing. If he is still dissatisfied, he may appeal to the Federal court. Once the verdict is pronounced, the person may not questioned it – whether he likes it or not. He has to accept that as *final*. What Scripture teaches is *final*. It may not be challenged, questioned, or contradicted. We have to accept it as the will of God. We have to submit to it. While a human court can be wrong and unfair, God cannot be wrong or unfair. We must accept the verdict of Scripture. The more willingly we submit ourselves to it, the happier we will be!

This, then, is what it means when we accept the Bible as the sole authority in all matters of faith and practice. We regard it as *complete, sufficient,* and *final*. Submission to God involves submission to His word. Love for God involves love for His word. That is why, whenever there is any controversy, or any uncertainty, we turn to the word of God. We will say, "To the law and to the testimony! If they do not speak according to this word, *it is* because *there is* no light in them" (Isaiah 8:20). The Bible decides!

1.2   The Perspicuity of Scripture

We often hear the objection being raised that different people have different interpretations of the Bible. By raising such an objection, it is implied that no one can claim he is right in his understanding of the Bible. It also implies that no one can be sure which is the right interpretation. If no one is sure which is the right interpretation, there is no need for anyone to follow the Bible! People are left to choose what they wish to believe. If that is the case, the authority of Scripture has been undermined. The individual is now the authority. *He* decides what *he* wants to follow!

This cannot be right. God has revealed His will to us in the Bible. If the Bible is really the revelation of God to us, it must be capable of being understood. Otherwise, how can it be the *revelation* of God? If it does not reveal God's will to us, it is not the revelation of God. For it to reveal God's will, it must be capable of being clearly understood. This is what has been called "the perspicuity of Scripture". What it means is basically that the Scripture is capable of being clearly understood. "All Scripture *is* given by inspiration of God, and *is* profitable for doctrine, for reproof, for correction, for instruction in righteousness, that the man of God may be complete, thoroughly equipped for every good work" (2 Timothy 3:16-17). If Scripture cannot be clearly understood, how is it going to be profitable to anyone? How can it reprove, correct and instruct? Scripture is capable of being clearly understood!

Capable of being clearly understood
Our lack of clarity in understanding any portion of Scripture must not be confused with the inherent perspicuity of Scripture. Scripture is capable of being clearly understood, but we may lack understanding of it because of personal limitations. Just because we are not clear about any doctrine does not mean that the Bible does not have clear teaching on that doctrine.

Take, for example, the doctrine of the Trinity. In the first three centuries after the apostles. Christians were troubled by wrong doctrines with regard to the Godhead. In order to refute those wrong doctrines, the early Christians had to clearly formulate what were right doctrines. They had, therefore, to wrestle with the teaching of the Bible. The Christian leaders had to meet often to discuss the matter. With time, the creeds were drawn up which expressed their findings. Today, we are able to state the doctrine of the Trinity without much difficulty, and we believe it to be a fundamental doctrine of the Bible.

The same thing is happening on some matters that Christians are disagreed about. As we study the Scripture, and interact with one another, the Holy Spirit wrestles with our spirits to lead us to a clearer understanding of the word of God. Some things might not be too clear to us now, but with time they will become clear. What is important is that we must believe that Scripture is capable of being clearly understood. And we must exert effort to study the word. It is as we prayerfully study the word of God that His Spirit leads us to an understanding of His truth.

Having said these, we must remember that the main things taught in the Bible may be clearly understood by anyone reading it with unprejudiced eyes. Martin Luther had to struggle with the doctrine of salvation, which for a long while was covered up by human traditions and Roman Catholic superstitions. We do not have to struggle the same way he did. We have only to listen to what he, and many other Christians like him, have discovered from the Bible. We examine their teaching in the light of the Bible, and find that salvation comes, indeed, by grace through faith in Christ alone, and not by the good works we perform. The same can be said about many other doctrines pertaining to God, the Christian life, and the church – they are clearly revealed in Scripture and may easily be understood.

The question that comes to us now is, "How may I understand Scripture correctly?" There are some basic rules of interpreting the Bible which we must follow.

Take the text plainly
Firstly, we must take the plain meaning of the words. Common sense and common practice tell us that this should be the way we read any text. For example, if the headline in the newspapers says "Tiger Kills Boy" we take it plainly to mean that an animal, namely a tiger, had killed a boy. We do not take it to mean that the Roman Catholic Church is attacking the Anglican Church! That would have been ridiculous. Communications between people will be impossible if we do not take words plainly. We will constantly be misinterpreting people, and we ourselves will constantly be misunderstood by others. Imagine what chaos, troubles and fighting will result!

The examples of Scripture also teach us this rule of "taking the text plainly". When the prophet Daniel read the writings of

Jeremiah, he understood the words plainly and believed that the exile of the Jews was coming to an end after seventy years (Daniel 9:2 cf. Jeremiah 25:11; 29:10). This was also the way the Lord understood Scripture. In Matthew 11:10, He applied the prophecy of Malachi to John the Baptist, which said. "Behold, I send My messenger before Your face, who will prepare Your way before You." While the prophecy itself did not state who the messenger was going to be, the meaning of the words were clear. The Lord understood the words plainly, and then applied that prophecy to John the Baptist. Another example is Matthew 13:14-17. There, the Lord understood the prophecy of Isaiah plainly. Verse 14 says. "Hearing you will hear and shall not understand, and seeing you will see and not perceive." In verse 16, He says, "But blessed *are* your eyes for they see, and your ears for they hear." The Lord did not give wild and fanciful interpretations to those words.

These are just random examples of how the words of Scripture were taken plainly.

It needs to be noted that "plainly" does not always mean "literally". Some passages of Scripture are plainly not literal. Take for example John 6:35, in which Jesus said, "I am the bread of life. He who comes to Me shall never hunger, and he who believes in Me shall never thirst." The Lord obviously did not mean He was a loaf of bread, to be literally munched and swallowed! Another example is Judges 9:8-15. There, Jotham said to the men of Shechem, "The trees once went forth to anoint a king over them. And they said to the olive tree, 'Reign over us!'..." It is obvious that this is figurative language. The meaning of the passage has to be sought from the context, which is our next rule.

Take the text in context
The second rule of interpretation is that we must take the text in context. Again, common sense and common practice demand this. Let us say you overhear someone shout, "Kill it!", at the same time that a cat runs out of the room. Without further investigation, you go straight to the police or the RSPCA

(the Royal Society for the Prevention of Cruelty to Animals) and report that some people are trying to kill a cat. If you had taken the trouble to just peer into the room, you would have discovered that the people in the room were attempting to kill a cockroach! You did hear the words, "Kill it!", but you have taken those words out of context.

Consider Matthew 27:5, which says, "Then he threw down the pieces of silver in the temple and departed, and went and hanged himself." Who hanged himself, and why? Imagine what ridiculous doctrine might possibly come out of this passage if we do not bother to check the context! It is the failure to check the context that has led some churches to practise feet-washing, based on John 13:1214. It is also the failure to understand a verse in context that has led the charismatics to claim that tongue-speaking may be practised for personal edification. They make this claim based on 1 Corinthians 14:4, which says, "He who speaks in a tongue edifies himself, but he who prophesies edifies the church." They have similarly misunderstood Mark 16:17, which says, "And these signs will follow those who believe: In My name they will cast out demons; they will speak with new tongues."

Compare scripture with scripture
The third rule is that we must compare scripture with scripture. Again this is a rule which we always use in everyday life, often without even thinking about it. Take, for example, the situation in which a man has left behind a will. One part of the will states that all his property is to be distributed to his children. When the property is being distributed, a cousin turns up and claims a share to it, saying that the word "children" can mean "relatives of the next generation". If the case is brought to court, the judge will go through the document to see how the word "children" is used elsewhere. Suppose he finds that in the first paragraph the names of the children are specified, and these are the immediate children of the deceased man. How do you think the judge will understand the word "children" in the paragraph that is controverted? Of course, the cousin will

lose his case!

That is the way we must interpret Scripture. One part must be compared with another which speaks of the same matter. Otherwise, we might get the doctrine wrong. For example, we read in 1 Corinthians 8:4, "Therefore concerning the eating of things offered to idols, we know that an idol is nothing in the world, and that *there is* no other God but one." From this we might draw the wrong conclusion that it is all right to eat food offered to idols, since "an idol is nothing in the world". However, we will draw a different conclusion when we consult 1 Corinthians 10:19-20, which says, "What am I saying then? That an idol is anything, or what is offered to idols is anything? Rather, that the things which the Gentiles sacrifice they sacrifice to demons and not to God, and I do not want you to have fellowship with demons."

You see now why it is so important to compare one part of Scripture with other parts. We know that our God is not a God of confusion. He will not contradict Himself by saying one thing in His word, and another thing in another part of His word.

These, then, are the basic rules of interpreting the Bible: take the text plainly, take the text in context, and compare scripture with scripture. By these three rules, we may come to a correct understanding of the Bible. This is because the Scripture may be clearly understood.

1.3   The Nature Of Revelation

The three basic rules of interpreting the Bible are enough for the average Christian to arrive at the correct understanding of a passage of Scripture. Books on how to interpret the Bible often give more rules than these three. The other rules, however, may be looked upon as refinements of the three basic ones we have learned – namely, to take the text plainly, to take the text in context, and to compare scripture with scripture.

We are concerned to know how Scripture should be interpreted because we believe that Scripture is the sole authority in all matters of faith and practice. Our understanding of the authority of Scripture in our lives will be enhanced if we understand the nature of revelation. Furthermore, the three basic rules of interpreting the Bible may be applied with greater facility if we understand how the different parts of the Bible relate to one another. Put another way, we wish to answer the questions, "How was Scripture given?", and "How do the different parts of the Bible relate to one another?"

The unity of God's word
The Bible was not dropped down from heaven complete. The prophets did not record the whole of the Bible at one sitting. Instead, God revealed His truth gradually, portion by portion, through the stages of the history of His people. When one part of the Bible was written down, it remained forever a part of God's word. When another portion of revelation was written down, the earlier portion did not become obsolete. One portion was added to another until the whole was complete.

The Bible is, in reality, a compilation of sixty-six books of various lengths. The first thirty-nine books, which form the Old Testament, are as much part of God's word as the twenty-seven books that form the New Testament. The process of revelation may be compared to the construction of a wall. The workers lay the bricks layer upon layer, so that all the layers are joined together to form a whole. All the bricks, and all the layers, may be liken to the different books and the different time in which they were written. Once complete, we see the wall as one solid slab. The later layers have been fused to the earlier layers, to form a complete wall.

The Old Testament and the New Testament *together* constitute God's word. We must not exalt one at the expense of the other. Throughout the history of the church, there have been many who did just that. We find this tendency prevalent among many good Christians today. Among Christians, the more common tendency is to exalt the New Testament above the Old. The claim is sometimes made that the Old Testament is obsolete. It has been superseded by the New. The New Testament is all that we need to live the Christian life. This, of course, is wrong because the whole of the Bible is God's word, not just the New Testament.

In the New Testament, we find many portions of the Old Testament quoted. The Lord quoted from the Old Testament, and so did the apostles. Our understanding of the New Testament will be deficient if we fail to see the significance of the Old Testament passages that are quoted. Moreover, we would have failed to see God as the God of history. We all know the importance of a sense of history. When a person does not know where he is from, he will have difficulty knowing where he is heading. He will not have a clear sense of purpose for his life. That is why we find that every great civilisation has a clear record of its history. That is why every strong nation will teach its people its own history.

What is the relationship between the Old and the New Testaments? Someone has stated it well: "The New Testament is in the Old concealed, and the Old Testament is by the New revealed." (Attributed to Augustine of Hippo (354-430 AD).) The way of salvation is clearly revealed to us in the New Testament. Jesus Christ is the way, the truth, and the life. Christ Jesus came into the world to save sinners. By His death on the cross of Calvary, He has borne the sins of all His people. He rose from death to give eternal life to all who repent of their sins and trust in Him. This message, however, is also contained in the Old Testament, although it is not so clearly stated. We see it, for example, in Genesis 3:15, "And I will put enmity between you and the woman, and between your seed and her Seed; He shall bruise your head, and you shall bruise His heel." This is widely recognised as a prophecy concerning the coming of Christ, who was "bruised in the heel" in His death, but who bruised Satan's head in His resurrection.

The teachings of the New Testament are concealed in the Old Testament, and the teachings of the Old Testament are revealed by the New Testament. We will have difficulty understanding the significance of the Old Testament sacrifices if it were not for the clearer revelation given to us in the book of

Hebrews. The Jews in the time of the apostles had difficulty understanding the prophecies concerning the coming Saviour, until the apostles persuaded them of Christ. The New Testament sheds light on the teachings of the Old Testament.

We see now the importance of holding to the unity of the Bible.

Progressive clarity and completeness
Since Scripture was given cumulatively and progressively, we must recognize that revelation became increasingly clear and complete. When interpreting the Scripture, we must not adopt a "static theology" in which no allowance is made for progression in revelation. This is a common mistake made by some good Christians. While other Christians have the tendency of exalting the New Testament above the Old, these have the tendency to adopt a "static theology". They mentally equate the Old Testament with the New. They then impose upon the Old Testament scriptures the teachings of the New Testament or, more commonly, they do the reverse of imposing upon the New Testament scriptures the teachings of the Old.

Since the New Testament came after the Old Testament, we naturally expect the teachings in the New Testament to be clearer. We also expect the practices established in the New Testament to be *normative*, that is, setting the norm for us to follow today. The Old Testament, for example, shows that the Jews were God's chosen people and He dealt with them as a nation (Deuteronomy 14:1-2). In the New Testament, the people of God are all who believe in Christ, and He deals with them as local churches (Hebrews 8:7-13; 2 Corinthians 6:16-18). In the Old Testament, adulterers were stoned to death. In the New Testament, corrective discipline is to be exercised in the churches (John 8:1-12; 1 Corinthians 5).

Even within each of the Testaments, progression is seen and must be recognised. In the Old Testament, prophecies of the coming Saviour became clearer and clearer with time. It also became clearer that true spirituality has nothing to do with natural descent nor with the keeping of religious rituals, and that God was going to call not only Jews, but also Gentiles, to be His people (Jeremiah 31:31-34; Isaiah 2:1-4; 42; 53; 60; etc.). When extended to the New Testament, we see it clearly taught in Galatians 3 that the true children of Abraham, the true people of God, are all those who have faith in Jesus Christ.

Progression of revelation is seen also within the New Testament. In John 16:13-15, the Lord promised the coming of the Holy Spirit, who will lead His disciples to further truths. We see this fulfilled in Acts 2, on the day of Pentecost, when the first New Testament church came into being. As local churches were established, elders were appointed (Acts 14:23). The pastoral epistles, which were written towards the end of Paul's life, give the qualifications of men who may be appointed to be elders and deacons (1 Timothy 3:1-13; Titus 1). The normative church order is thus established.

We see a similar unfolding of the Great Commission of Matthew 28: 18-20. The Old Testament had prophesied the salvation of the Gentiles. We see now how this is to be accomplished. The Lord had foretold, before His death and resurrection, that He would draw all nations to Himself when He was lifted up (John 12:32). The resurrected Christ now gave this commission to His disciples. This command is repeated in Acts 1:8, with the explicit description that the gospel is to be preached farther and farther afield, in a widening circle. The travels of Philip and Peter (Acts 8:5; 9:32ff.), and the missionary journeys of Paul, confirm to us the right understanding of the Great Commission – that it is a command given to local churches, to plant other local churches, to establish them in the teachings of the Lord, and to be carried out for all time.

Once this truth is grasped – namely, that the word of God was given with increasing clarity and completeness – we will not fall into the trap of equating the Old Testament with the New. We will not commit the error of resurrecting the Passover feast to be celebrated by Christians today, as has happened in a church in Malaysia. The Passover feast pointed to Christ's sacrificial death on the cross, and is not to be celebrated by Christians anymore (1 Corinthians 5:7-8; Hebrews 10:10, 18).

Instead, we celebrate the Lord's Supper, which is a new ordinance of the new covenant. We will not have "tarrying meetings", hoping for a repetition of Pentecost, in which the sound of roaring wind was heard and tongues of fire seen. That belonged to the transition period between the old dispensation and the new, when the first New Testament churches were born. We will also not be surprised to learn that the Scripture actually teaches the cessation of the revelatory gifts when, the revelation of God was completed (1 Corinthians 13:8-13). We know that the revelation of God to us became complete with the writing of the last book of the Bible – the book of Revelation.

These, then, are the implications of the truth that Scripture was given cumulatively and progressively – firstly, we must hold to the unity of Scripture; and secondly, we must understand that God's word was given with increasing clarity and completeness.

1.4   Conclusion

We must complete this study on the authority of by drawing three practical conclusions.

Trust the word
Firstly, we must trust the word of God. The word of God is described as "the sword of the Spirit" in Ephesians 6:17. We are commanded to put on the whole armour of God so that we may be able to stand against the wiles of the devil. Of all the pieces of armour mentioned, this is the only one that is offensive in nature. God has provided us not only the defensive weapons but also this offensive one. Otherwise, like the soldier in battle, we will be shot at, hit, poked and knocked down often by the devil, with no offensive weapon at hand to keep him off. Like our Lord, when He was tempted in the wilderness by the devil (Matthew 4:1-11), we are able to use the sword of the Spirit to drive away our adversary.

Imagine now that in the midst of a particularly fierce battle, your sword crosses that of the adversary. You hear a sharp snap and realises that a sword is broken. As you look down on the ground you find, indeed, the blade of a broken sword. As you look at your hand, to your horror you discover that it is your own sword that is broken! We do not want such a situation to happen to us. We do not wish to wield an untrustworthy sword – not in the midst of our spiritual struggle with the devil! Thank God, the sword He has equipped us with is a trustworthy one. His word is sure and true. It will not fail us. All Scripture is given by inspiration of God. We must trust His word!

Study the word

Secondly, we must make every effort to study the word of God. What is the use of keeping our Bible nicely displayed on the shelf? The Bible is meant to be read. Scripture is capable of being clearly understood. If no effort is made to understand the word of God, no good will come to us. We know that the Holy Spirit works by the word. He enlightens us to understand the word, and He works in us by the word. Those who do not exert effort to study the word cannot expect to have the blessings of the Spirit of God.

The Lord declares that man shall not live by bread alone, but by every word that proceeds from the mouth of God (Matt. 4:4). The Bible also tells us that every believer is expected to become a teacher of the word – some perhaps to become preachers, others to become Sunday schools teachers, and all of us to be able to instruct our children (Hebrews 5:12-14). If effort is not made to study the Bible, if time is not spent reading the Bible daily, if you do not come to church regularly to hear the word of God proclaimed, how are you ever to grow to spiritual maturity?

Live according to the word

Trust the word we must! Study the word we must! Do not forget, next, the importance of living according to the word. There are too many people who profess faith in Christ, but do not live according to His word. There are others who spoil their witness to the unbelieving world by their inconsistent life. When a Christian fails to live up to what he professes to believe in, he will not make an impact upon his unconverted friends. How we need to grow in the grace and the knowledge of our Lord and Saviour Jesus Christ (2 Peter 3:18)! If you love the Lord, you will keep His word (John 14:21-24).

This applies to the church as much as it applies to the individual Christian. If the Scripture is the sole authority in all matters of faith and practice, we will not want to insist upon our own opinions and our traditional practices. We will want to follow the teaching of the Bible, and discard all man-made methods of worship and church government. This is what has been called *the Regulative Principle*. We allow the Bible to regulate our lives.

Trust the word of God! Study the word of God! Live according to the word of God!

Two

THE CHURCH IS ONE BODY (1 Corinthians 12:1-31)

In this first letter to the Corinthians, the apostle Paul deals with various problems that the church was facing: for example, sectarianism, immorality, a believer suing another in the law court, and food offered to idols. One of the problems faced by the Corinthian church was the exercise of spiritual gifts in public worship. The gifts of prophecy and tongues, and especially tongues, are singled out. There was disorder, chaos and disagreement concerning the use of these gifts in public worship. This is exactly the problem we are observing in many of today's churches. To find the solution to the problem we are facing today, we must come back to the Scriptures and determine what they teach about this matter.

Of the many passages in the Bible that are relevant to this subject, the 1 Corinthians passage is the fullest. We must therefore make a careful study of this passage before we consider the others. We must note that Chapters 12, 13 and 14 belong together. All three chapters deal with the one subject of the use of "the sign gifts" in public worship. Remember that the original Bible did not have chapter and verse divisions. The chapter and verse divisions were added by scholars to help us in the study of the Bible.

Paul was a great teacher. In this letter, he deals with some important underlying principles before coming to the problem of "the gifts". We can see the wisdom of this. By dealing with the underlying principles first, he knows that the readers will be more convinced of the practical instructions later. We see this operating in everyday-life. If you tell your children to finish their homework before dinner, they will do it if they are already trained to be obedient. But they might be wondering why it is that they have to finish their homework early today. However, if you tell them that you are taking the family out after dinner, they are more likely to finish their homework with greater willingness and joy. Understanding the reasons behind the practical instructions will help so much in securing obedience (cf. John 15:15). Furthermore, when the underlying principles were understood, the readers would be able to apply them to some other similar situations, and not just to the immediate problem.

The first basic principle is taught in this chapter of 1 Corinthians. Other important principles are given in 1 Corinthians 13 and 14, before practical instructions are given on how tongues and prophecies are to be used in public worship. Here, in 1 Corinthians 12, the apostle wishes to emphasise the truth that *the church is one body*. This truth is developed in three basic sections. Verses 1 to 11 form the first section, in which is taught the truth that *there is unity in diversity*. Verses 14 to 31 form the last section, in which is taught the truth that *there is diversity in unity*. These two sections are connected by the middle one, which is made up of verses 12 and 13. This middle section acts very much like the spine of a book, which connects the front cover to the back cover. It teaches the truth that the body is one. It is this truth, in the middle section, which gives unity to the whole chapter. That is why we say that this chapter emphasizes the one important principle, namely that *the church is one body*.

2.1   There Is Unity In Diversity (12:1-11)

Act like true Christians!
Let us come to the first section of this chapter. Remember that Chapters 12, 13 and 14 belong together. The first three verses of Chapter 12 therefore serve as the introduction, not only to this chapter, but also to the whole passage, from Chapter 12 to Chapter 14. Paul begins by saying, "Now concerning spiritual *gifts*, brethren, I do not want you to be ignorant" (12:1). Note what Paul is saying; he says, "...I do not want you to be ignorant". He is here emphasising the importance of knowledge, in order that errors may be dispelled. This is a typical emphasis of the apostle. He said virtually the same thing in the earlier chapters, when dealing with other problems. In Chapter 10, verse I, he said, "Moreover, brethren, I do not want you to be unaware..." In Chapter 11, verse 3, he said, "But I want you to know..." In Colossians 2:1, the same apostle said, "For I want you to know..."

When faced with error of any kind, it is important to know the correct teaching with regard to the matter at stake. Otherwise, we will never be sure of what is right and what is wrong. And when we are not sure, we will not be able to steer clear of the error, let alone to counter it. We are currently faced with the errors of the Charismatic movement. How can we be sure that the Charismatics are wrong? We can be sure only by coming to the Scriptures to see what is taught there. We must face the issue, and make effort to study what the Scriptures teach on the subject. Retreat is never the solution. When you try to run away from the problem, it will continue to dog you. If you face it, however, there is the possibility of becoming clear about the matter. When you are clear, you will have peace of mind. You will not be troubled by the "problem" any more, since it will no longer be a problem to you. You will then be in a position to help others who have the same problem.

The apostle moves on to say that he is dealing with converted people: "You know that you were Gentiles, carried away to these dumb idols, however you were led" (12:2). This is, again, a typical approach of the apostle. He always reminds his readers what they were before, and what they are now. We see this, for example, in Ephesians 2:1-6. There, he reminds the Ephesians that they were once "dead in trespasses and sins", they once "walked according to the course of this world", but now they have been made alive by Christ. In 1 Thessalonians 1:9, he reminds his readers how they "turned to God from idols to serve the living and true God..." The purpose of reminding his readers of what they once were and what they now are is to jolt them to the realization that they must behave as new creatures. They must act like Christians, and not like unconverted people.

The Corinthians were once pagans. They did not use their mind to think. They were simply carried away to dumb idols by their traditions and prejudices; they were led about without correct knowledge. But they are different now. They once called Jesus accursed, but now they trust in Him as Lord. "Therefore I make known to you that no one speaking by the Spirit of God calls Jesus accursed, and no one can say that Jesus is Lord except by the Holy Spirit" (12:3).

Taking the three verses together, Paul is saying to his readers that in the matter of spiritual gifts, they must *act like true Christians, and be guided by correct knowledge!*

Gifts are from God
The general introduction has been given. The apostle now makes the point that *all gifts come from the same God.* He says, in verses 4 to 6, "There are diversities of gifts, but the same Spirit. There are differences of ministries, but the same Lord. And there are diversities of activities, but it is the same God who works all in all." What he is saying is basically that there may be different abilities seen among church members, but they all come from the same God. Call them "gifts" (*charismata*) if you like, they all come from the same Spirit (verse 4). Call them "ministries", or "services", if you like, they all come from the same Lord (verse 5). Call them "activities" if you like, they all come from the same God (verse 6). In short, all abil-

ities come from the same triune God – Father, Son and Holy Spirit. None can boast that he is better than others, because whatever gifts or abilities he has come not from himself but from God.

Gifts are to profit all
The next point he makes is that *the different abilities are meant to profit all in the church*. It says, in verse 7, "But the manifestation of the Spirit is given to each one for the profit *of all*". Here, "the manifestation of the Spirit" is a reference to the many gifts or abilities spoken of in the earlier verses. Examples of these gifts are listed in the verses following. The Spirit is invisible, but His working in God's people may be seen publicly. That is why the gifts of the Spirit are a "manifestation".

It says, in verses 8-11, "for to one is given the word of wisdom through the Spirit, to another the word of knowledge through the same Spirit, to another faith by the same Spirit, to another gifts of healings by the same Spirit, to another the working of miracles, to another prophecy, to another discerning of spirits, to another *different* kinds of tongues, to another the interpretation of tongues. But one and the same Spirit works all these things, distributing to each one individually as He wills." This list of gifts is not exhaustive. There are other gifts of the Spirit mentioned in verses 28 to 30 of the same chapter which are not mentioned here. Other passages of the New Testament, such as Romans 12:6-8 and Ephesians 4:11, also mention gifts that are not found here. For example, the Romans 12 passage mentions the gifts of leading, giving and showing mercy that are not found in 1 Corinthians 12. This goes to show that the gifts mentioned in 1 Corinthians 12:8-11 are meant only as examples of the "manifestation of the Spirit" that was referred to in verse 7.

Since these gifts are meant only to illustrate the sort of things the apostle is referring to, we should not be too obsessed with determining what exactly each of them is. We should not be side-tracked from the main issues which the apostle wants to bring across to us here, in this chapter. As long as we know what he means by "spiritual gifts" (verse 1), as long as we know what he means by "the manifestation of the Spirit" (verse 7), it is sufficient for the purpose at the moment.

Gifts are distributed as the Spirit wills
While we must not dwell on the details, we must not miss the main points either. There are a couple of points that he is emphasising here. He has already said, in verse 7, that all spiritual gifts are meant for the profit of all. Another point he is emphasising is that all these *gifts are distributed according to the sovereign will of the Spirit of God.* This is clear from verse 11, "But one and the same Spirit works all these things, distributing to each one individually as He wills." You see now how the apostle turns the attention of the Corinthian Christians away from themselves to God and His church. There is a tendency in fallen men to be inward looking. The apostle wants Christians to behave differently – to look not to themselves, but to the need of others.

The apostle had begun by urging us to *act like true Christians, and be guided by correct knowledge.* Concerning spiritual gifts, he has three things to say about them. Firstly, *all spiritual gifts come from the triune God* (vs. 4-6). The gifts do not come from the individuals, nor belong to the individuals, who have them. Secondly, *all spiritual gifts are meant for the profit of the church.* They are not meant to benefit only the individuals who possess them. Thirdly, the *gifts are distributed according to the sovereign will of God.* They are not given because certain individuals are in some ways better than others, nor are they given simply because they have been asked for. The diversity of gifts and individuals are drawn together, as it were, by the triune God to form the church. *There is unity in diversity.*

This unity, or oneness, of the body is discussed next by the apostle.

2.2   The Body Is One (12:12-13)

Verses 12 to 13 say, "For as the body is one and has many members, but all the members of that one body, being many, are one body, so also *is* Christ. For by one Spirit we were all baptised into one body – whether Jews or Greeks, whether slaves or free – and have all been made to drink into one Spirit."

What is the body spoken of here, and in other verses of this chapter? We have assumed that it is a reference to the church. The context requires that we understand it as such. In this letter, Paul was addressing the local church in Corinth. In verse 27 of the present chapter, he says, "Now you are the body of Christ, and members individually." In verse 28, he plainly declares, "And God has appointed these in the church..." From these considerations, we are convinced that Paul is referring primarily to the local church. He is referring to the Corinthian church in particular, and other local churches in general.

Local churches, however, are the manifestation of the universal, invisible, church of Jesus Christ. The universal church is made up of believers from all ages. Many of them are now in glory, others are found in all parts of the world, and yet others will be called out of the world through the preaching of the gospel. It is God's purpose that when a believer is called out of the world, he is to become a member of a local church. He becomes a member of the universal church of Jesus Christ from the moment he is converted, and he should join himself to a good local church somewhere.

These are the only two ways the word "church", or *ecclesia* in Greek, is used in the New Testament. It is a reference either to the universal church, or to local churches. Since local churches are the manifestation of the universal church on earth, we should not be surprised if Paul switches the discussion from one to the other. The two are intimately linked together. The characteristics of the universal church should be reflected in the life of the local church. Paul has been addressing the Corinthians as a local church, but he now links them to the universal church. This he does in verses 12 and 13. In verse 12, he refers first to the local church, saying, "For as the body is one and has many members, but all the members of that one body, being many, are one body,..." He then links it to the universal church by saying, "so also is Christ". Verse 13 then goes on to talk about certain truths connected with the universal church that are true also of the local church.

We say that verse 13 is, strictly speaking, a reference to the universal church because the same apostle referred to it as "the body of Christ" in Ephesians 5. He says, in Ephesians 5:23, "For the husband is head of the wife, as also Christ is head of the church; and He is the Saviour of the body." He goes on to say, in Ephesians 5:25-27, "Husbands, love your wives, just as Christ also loved the church and gave Himself for her, that He might sanctify and cleanse her with the washing of water by the word, that He might present her to Himself a glorious church, not having spot or wrinkle or any such thing, but that she should be holy and without blemish." The church referred to here is the universal church. We see, then, that Paul, in 1 Corinthians 12:12-13, is comparing the local church with the universal church. In verse 13, he is drawing out some truths concerning the universal church to apply to the local church which is referred to in verse 12, and elsewhere in this chapter. Let us now see what Paul has to say in these two verses.

In verse 12, Paul tells us that the local church may be compared to the human body, which has many different parts, or "members". Although the parts are many, they make up one, and only one, body. The emphasis is on the oneness of the body. This oneness is to be expected since, in the universal church, which is the one body of Christ, there are diverse members. We are told, in verse 13, that in the body of Christ, people of various ethnic backgrounds and various social standings make up its membership – "whether Jews or Greeks, whether slaves or free".

Paul is, of course, talking about spiritual oneness – a oneness that has been brought about by the Holy Spirit. He says, "For by one Spirit we were all baptised into one body... and have all been made to drink into one Spirit." He is taking for granted that all his readers know that union with the Holy Spirit takes place at conversion. Sad to say, this is not the case today. Not everyone knows that a person receives the Holy Spirit at his conversion. In fact, many have been taught that a believer still needs to be "baptised by/in/with the Holy Spirit" some time after his conversion. We must therefore prove the truth that the Holy Spirit is received on conversion.

In Galatians 3:2, Paul asks the rhetorical question, "This only I want to learn from you: Did you receive the Spirit by the works of the law, or by the hearing of faith?" A rhetorical question is a question whose answer is obvious. Here, the answer is obviously, "By the hearing of faith." Clearly, a person receives the Spirit when he comes to faith in Christ. We know that "the hearing of faith" is a reference to conversion because the same apostle says, in Romans 10:17, "faith comes by hearing, and hearing by the word of God". The Holy Spirit is received when a person is converted. It is impossible to be a Christian without the Holy Spirit living in you. It says in Romans 8:9, "But you are not in the flesh but in the Spirit, if indeed the Spirit of God dwells in you. Now if anyone does not have the Spirit of Christ, he is not His." Again, in verse 11, "But if the Spirit of Him who raised Jesus from the dead dwells in you, He who raised Christ from the dead will also give life to your mortal bodies through His Spirit who dwells in you."

Note, by the way, that the same sort of language is employed in Romans 8:9 and 11 as in 1 Corinthians 12:13. In the Romans passage, the believer is "in the Spirit" at the same time that the Spirit dwells in him. In 1 Corinthians 12:13, we were baptised by the Spirit and we have been made to drink into one Spirit, which is the same as saying that we are in the Spirit and the Spirit is in us. It is normally impossible for one thing in be in another at the same time that the other is in the one. An illustration might help us understand this concept, however. If a bucket is immersed in the sea, we can say that the water is in the bucket at the same time that the bucket is in the water! This, however, is only an illustration, which comes far short of the spiritual reality that the Bible is teaching. What is being taught is that we receive the Holy Spirit, and become united to Christ, at the point of our conversion.

The thrust of 1 Corinthians 12:13 must not be lost. It is the oneness of the body of Christ that is being emphasized. "For by one Spirit we were all baptised into one body... and have all been made to drink into one Spirit." What Paul is saying in this section is that just as the body of Christ is one despite being made up of diverse members, so also *the local church is one body although made up of many members*.

2.3   There Is Diversity In Unity (12:14-31)

We come to the last section of this chapter, which comprises verses 14 to 31. Here, the truth is established that *there is diversity in unity*.

No place for discontent or envy
This last section begins with a repetition of the truth, "For in fact the body is not one member but many," in verse 14. This is followed by, "If the foot should say, 'Because I am not a hand, I am not of the body,' is it therefore not of the body? And if the ear should say, 'Because I am not an eye, I am not of the body,' is it therefore not of the body?" (verses 15-16). Here is a case of discontent and envy. The foot envies the hand, and the ear envies the eye. The foot is not content with what God has made it to be, and so is the ear. We do meet with such individuals in the church. They think they are worse off than others. They think they are not as useful as others. They become discontented with themselves, and begin to envy others who appear to have more gifts, or who appear to be more greatly used by God. They begin to dissociate themselves from the life of the church, claiming that they are not important. They say that the church can continue to function well without them. They speak as though they are so humble when, in reality, they a discontented with themselves and are envious of

others. Beware! God knows your heart. And, often, others are able to see through your pretended humility.

Let us think and act in a more mature way. By pretending not to be part of the body, do we really cease to be part of the body? Such thinking is ridiculous! When the foot or the ear says that it is not part of the body, does it cease to be part of the body? You know that it is impossible for you to cease being a part of the body of Christ, unless of course, you turn out to be an apostate! Only a person who is not a true Christian will eventually drop away from the church of Christ. This truth is clearly taught in Hebrews 6:4-6, "For it is impossible for those who were once enlightened, and have tasted the heavenly gift, and have become partakers of the Holy Spirit, and have tasted the good word of God and the powers of the age to come, if they fall away, to renew them again to repentance, since they crucify again for themselves the Son of God, and put Him to an open shame."

Coming back to the 1 Corinthians 12 passage, we imagine an eye growing bigger and bigger, at the same time that the other parts of the body grow smaller and smaller, until they disappear. What we would have then is a giant eye! "If the whole body *were* an eye, where *would be* the hearing?" The same can be said of the ear, or any other part of the body. "If the whole *were* hearing, where *would be* the smelling? But now God has set the members, each one of them, in the body just as He pleased" (verses 17-18). The sovereign will of God is put forth again, as in verse 11. It is God who has made each one of us the way he is. We have no right to mourn. We have no right to be discontented with ourselves or to be envious of others.

No place for pride or arrogance
We move on to the next point. Just as there is no place for discontent or envy in the church, there is also no place for pride or arrogance. This Paul shows from verse 20 to the first part of verse 24. Those who are prone to discontent or envy like to think of themselves as not needed in the church, while those who are prone to pride or arrogance like to think that they

alone are important in the church. Imagine what will happen to the church when both groups are present at the same time. One group wishes to dissociate itself from the circle of the church, and the other group wishes to shrink the circle of the church. The rift between the two groups will become very wide indeed! To the first group, who are prone to discontent or envy, Paul has given the reminder that the body is not one member but many (verse 14). In other words, they are important to the well-being of the church. To the second group, who are prone to pride or arrogance, Paul now says that there are many members, yet one body (verse 20). In other words, they are not the only ones who are important in the church.

He elaborates this point by saying, "And the eye cannot say to the hand, 'I have no need of you'; nor again the head to the feet, 'I have no need of you.' No, much rather, those members of the body which seem to be weaker are necessary. And those members of the body which we think to be less honourable, on these we bestow greater honour" (verses 21-23). The, eye may be weaker than the hand, but it is very necessary to the proper functioning of the wholes body. Similarly, the head may not be as physically strong as the feet, but it is absolutely necessary to the living person. The eyes and the head are, therefore, regarded as more important, or as possessing more honour. However, the hands and the feet, which we think are less honourable, receive more attention from us. Others may not pay much attention to our hands and feet, but we do. We would wear gloves when necessary, and we would wear shoes most of the time. In fact, we would cover up the unseemly parts of the body all the more, in order to give to them a dignity not needed by the comely parts. "And our unpresentable *parts* have greater modesty, but our presentable *parts* have no need" (verses 23-24). Yes, even the private parts of the body are important, for they are necessary for procreation.

Thus far, figures of speech have been used. Paul has been talking about the human body and its many parts. He now begins to speak more plainly, in verses 24 to 27, about the body, which is the local church – "But God composed the body, having given greater honour to that *part* which lacks it, that there should be no schism in the body, but *that* the members should have the same care for one another." His basic message here is that the unity of the church must be preserved and manifested. Instead of competing with one another, there should be mutual care between the church members. After all, we share the same life. "And if one member suffers, all the members suffer with *it*; or if one member is honoured, all the members rejoice with *it*" (v. 26). We know this in real life. If a foot steps on a nail, it is not only the foot that is hurt, but the whole body. When a member of the church suffers, we all suffer together because we share the same spiritual life in Christ. And within the local church, we feel it all the more because all the members have covenanted together to be a church-family. Conversely, when a member is honoured, we all rejoice together. Who will not rejoice if his brother or sister is honoured in some way in society? Just as in the family, so also in the church – only a small- hearted and perverse person will not rejoice when a fellow church member is honoured!

Just in case you have missed the point and are still not clear about all that has been said so far concerning the body and its members, Paul says, "Now you are the body of Christ, and members individually" (v. 27). *You* are the people I am referring to, not others.

How these truths relate to spiritual gifts
Paul now relates all he has been saying about the members of the body to the issue of spiritual gifts. He says, in verse 28, "And God has appointed these in the church: first apostles, second prophets, third teachers, after that miracles, then gifts of healings, helps, administrations, varieties of tongues." A few observations must be made.

Firstly, we observe that there is an order of importance in the gifts. Deliberately, Paul lists them in order – "*first* apostles, *second* prophets, *third* teachers, *after that* miracles, *then* gifts of healings..." The apostle does not hold to the mistaken idea that everyone in the church must be absolutely equal before there can be unity.

Secondly, we note that the greater gifts are, in fact, the teaching gifts. Apostles, prophets and teachers are mentioned before all the other gifts, showing that those whose duty it is to make known the will of God are regarded as more important. The first part of verse 28 reminds us that it is God who has appointed these in the church.

Thirdly, we note that of all the gifts, tongues is listed last! This is significant, in view of the fact that this was the gift most controverted in the Corinthian church. We should take note of this fact today.

A series of rhetorical questions follows in verses 29 to 30, all of which require the answer, "No!" "*Are* all apostles? *Are* all prophets? *Are* all teachers? *Are* all workers of miracles? Do all have gifts of healings? Do all speak with tongues? Do all interpret?" The obvious answer to all these questions is, "No!" This underlines the truth that there are many members, with diverse gifts, in the church.

The chapter ends with the words, "But earnestly desire the best gifts. And yet I show you a more excellent way" (v. 31). We already know what are the best, or greater, gifts. They are the teaching gifts. There are no more apostles and prophets around today. This we will show in a latter chapter of this book. Only the office of teacher remains. To desire the best gift today is to desire to be a teacher of the word. It is to desire to be a pastor. Why then should people be clamouring for the gift of tongues, as though that is the most important gift? As for "the more excellent way", Paul shows what it is in the next chapter of 1 Corinthians.

2.4   Some Conclusions

Errors of the Charismatics
From this study of 1 Corinthians 12, we are now able to see where the so-called Charismatic movement has gone wrong.

We note, firstly, that the Charismatics are wrong in emphasising experience at the expense of truth. Their emphasis on experience – on what they feel, or what has happened to them – is contradicted by verses 1 to 3, verse 28, and verse 31. All these verses emphasise the importance of truth, of doctrine, of correct knowledge.

Secondly, the Charismatics are wrong in teaching a post-conversion baptism of the Spirit. Their claim is that when converted, the person still needs the "baptism of/with/by/in the Spirit" to make him a better Christian. This teaching is contradicted by verse 13, which teaches that the baptism of/with/by/in the Spirit occurs at conversion.

Thirdly, the Charismatics are wrong in teaching that the proof of your Spirit baptism is tongue-speaking. This is contradicted by verses 4 to 6, 11, 18 and 30. These verses show that it is God who sovereignly distributes the gifts according to His will, and that not all have the same gifts. All other gifts are also "the manifestation of the Spirit".

Fourthly, the Charismatics are wrong in claiming that the gift of tongues is for personal edification while other gifts are for edifying the church. This is contradicted by v. 7, and also by Chapter 14:26, which we shall come to in a later study. Verse 7 of Chapter 12 shows that all gifts are meant for the profit of all.

Fifthly... "Enough! Enough!", you might say. But we have not finished yet. There is another characteristic of the Charismatic movement we must point out, and it is this. The Charismatics are wrong in advocating unity among believers and churches at the expense of truth but, along the way, creating so much disunity. It is a well-known fact that wherever the Charismatic movement has influenced a church, division has resulted. At the same time, the Charismatic movement is uniting people of diverse and questionable beliefs and practices – Roman Catholics included. These are contradicted by verses 1 to 3 which stress the importance of truth, and by verse 25 which teaches that there should be no division in the church.

Many Charismatics who hear or read a message like this one will want to say that they do not subscribe to all the characteristics of the Charismatic movement recorded here. We recognise the fact that not all Charismatics are the same; that some are more extreme than others. It cannot be denied, however, that these characteristics are generally true of what is now called the Charismatic movement. Whether or not you are an "extreme Charismatic" is not the point here. What is important is whether you are associated with it at all, whether you hold to any of the characteristics we have described above.

We take no pleasure in pointing out the errors of the Charismatics. But we have to do it because, otherwise, we would be unfaithful to the Lord and His word. Our purpose is to explain what we believe to be correct biblical teaching. Our aim is to follow the teaching of Scripture. A Christian is a follower of Christ, and the Bible is the revelation of Christ. If Jesus Christ is your Lord, you will want to follow what His word teaches. If you are a true disciple of Christ, you will want to throw away whatever practice that is contrary to His word.

Unity and edification
We have applied this passage to the Charismatic movement. We must now apply it to ourselves. We do not wish to be good only at pointing out the errors of others, forgetting about ourselves. What has this chapter to teach us? This study has shown that the body of Christ is one. All gifts of the Spirit are meant to profit the whole body. We must not allow sinful attitudes and actions to disrupt the unity of the body. Two questions are in order.

The first question we must ask is, are you – by your words, deeds or attitude – causing division to the church? This is intensely personal. We must examine our own hearts. If you are in any way causing division in the body of Christ, you should quickly repent. Otherwise, the Lord will chastise you, unless you are not His true children. This is the teaching in Hebrews 12:3-11. Verse 8 says, "But if you are without chastening, of which all have become partakers, then you are illegitimate and not sons." God will pursue His sinning children until they repent. Those who are not His children, He leaves to wallow in their sins. The sooner you turn away from your sins, and return to Him, the happier you will be!

The second question we must ask is, are you making positive efforts to build up the church and maintain its unity? It is one thing to believe in the importance of edification and church unity. It is another thing to work at edifying the church. Positive efforts are needed. There are many things that can be done. You can get to know other members of the church better. You can utter good things about your brothers and sisters in Christ instead of saying bad things about them when they are not around. You can attend the various meetings of the church instead of absenting yourselves. By not attending church meetings, you not only lose out yourselves, but become a discouragement to others. You also become a discouragement to the pastor. Yes, the pastor needs encouragement as well! We know what it is like to find one brother or one sister absent from the reunion dinner during Chinese New Year. Perhaps he or she is unable to come home because of the distance. Whatever the reason may be, you feel his or her absence! You know that the family is not complete! The same may be said about the church. Every time a member is absent, we sense that the church family is not complete! You must work at edifying others.

The church is one body!

Three

THE MORE EXCELLENT WAY (1 Corinthians 13:1-13)

We know that many people today are caught up in the Charismatic movement. It is important for us to be able to show them from the Bible where they have gone wrong. The Bible is alone the authority in all matters of faith and practice. We know that God's word cannot be wrong, but men can be wrong. The Bible is alone sufficient to show us the correct way. We must turn to the Bible to find out God's will for us.

In the time of the apostle Paul, the church at Corinth was faced with the problem of having people who were too keen about prophecy and tongues. This is exactly the problem faced by many churches today. We have seen that Paul deals with the problem by laying down some important principles first. He will discuss how spiritual gifts are to be used in public worship later. His chief concern at the moment is to lay down some foundational truths that are relevant to the subject. In Chapter 12 of 1 Corinthians, he has laid down the truth that *the church is one body*. Nothing sinful or selfish should be done to divide the one body of Christ. Paul ended that chapter by saying, "And yet I show you more excellent way."

What is that more excellent way? Here, in Chapter 13, Paul wishes to show us that that way is the way of love. He is actually making a slight digression from the main theme, which is the use of spiritual gifts in public worship. It is as though he is leading us on a slight detour from the main road so that we may see the beauty of the trees and the flowers along the road. He will take us back to the main road again soon enough, but it is important for us to appreciate the beauty of the flowers and trees along the main road. By making such a detour, he is in fact laying down another foundational truth relevant to the whole subject of spiritual gifts. He is going to show to us that all our spiritual gifts amount to nothing if there is no love seen in us. In fact, he discusses love together with other Christian graces and contrasts them with spiritual gifts. Put another way, he wishes to show the importance of *graces*, which have to do with our character, as contrasted with *gifts*, which have to do with our abilities. So then, *Christian graces* are contrasted with *spiritual gifts*; our *character* is contrasted with our *abilities*.

3.1   Love Is Indispensable (13:1-3)

This chapter divides naturally into three sections. The first three verses teach us the main truth that *love is indispensable*. We cannot do without love. If there is no love in us, everything else is worthless. Throughout this section, Paul uses *hyperbole*, which is a rhetorical exaggeration. In other words, he is using superlative, exaggerated, language to bring home a point.

Angelic languages?
He says in verse 1, "Though I speak with the tongues of men and of angels, but have not love, I have become sounding brass or a clanging cymbal." Paul is here not saying that he, or any other men, can speak in the language of angels. He is only saying that all our abilities at speaking the different languages, whether of men or of angels, amount to nothing if we have not love. All our speaking will be as useless as the sounds of metal instruments. That is plainly what Paul is saying. Plain as that is, there are those who would wrest this verse out of context

and claim that their "tongue speaking" is in fact the uttering of angelic languages! What are the languages of angels? How do they sound like? Have you heard them before? None of us know what angelic languages are like. Anyone can therefore come to us and utter some gibberish which they claim to be angelic languages. But why in the first place should men be uttering angelic speech? What purpose does it serve? Do they become angelic by so doing? Or are they becoming more "chimpanzeeic"?

In 2 Corinthians 12:2, Paul says this, "I know a man in Christ who fourteen years ago – whether in the body I do not know, or whether out of the body I do not know, God knows – such a one was caught up to the third heaven." He goes on to say in verse 4, "...he was caught up into Paradise and heard inexpressible words, which is not lawful for a man to utter." Paul was here countering his opponents who boasted of their spiritual experiences. He was relating his own experiences, but refused to say so directly. He knew that there is a limit to boasting, even of the right kind. He could have said, "I have greater experiences than you," but he chose not to do so. Instead, he put it in the third person, saying, "I know a man in Christ who had these experiences..."

Take note that Paul heard "inexpressible words". The question that may be raised is this – Was it the words themselves that were inexpressible, or was it the content of the words that was inexpressible? Let us take the first possibility. If Paul heard words that were inexpressible, if he heard angels speaking angelic languages, then he clearly tells us that it is not lawful for man to utter such angelic languages on earth. The Charismatics would be wrong in claiming that man can speak angelic languages on earth!

Consider the next possibility. If it is the content of what he heard that was inexpressible then it still follows that Paul understood what the angels were saying, between themselves or to him. In the Bible, we find that every time God or an angel speak to men, they do so in languages that could be understood. The same happened to Paul when he was taken in the spirit to heaven. He heard words that he could understand. If this is the case, then Paul is saying that the content of what he heard was too lofty to be uttered on earth.

You see then that, either way, the Charismatics are in trouble. If the "inexpressible words" refers to the *languages* of angels, then it is not lawful for Charismatics to be uttering them on earth. If it refers to the content of the words, then Paul understood what he heard, in a language. The words he heard were not mere sounds. Instead, they had meanings, and were arranged together in such a way that they constituted a language which conveyed intelligible ideas. This is so different from the claims of the Charismatics who utter nothing but mere gibberish. There is no syntax, there is no grammar, there is no sentence structure in the sounds that they utter. Language experts have analysed their so-called tongues but found that they are not languages at all! The Charismatics themselves do not understand what they are uttering. That is for the simple reason that the sounds that come out of their mouths do not constitute a language!

Paul is using exaggerated, high-flown words, to bring home the point that love is indispensable. It is not wrong for him to do so. In life, we express ourselves in different ways. We sometimes use a proverb. We sometimes use a comparison. We sometimes use a question, even though we already know the answer. Paul is not saying that men can speak angelic languages, nor that men can know everything, nor that men can remove mountains. Verses 2 and 3 make sense only when we understand them in the same way that we have understood verse 1: "And though I have *the gift of* prophecy, and understand all mysteries and all knowledge, and though I have all faith, so that I could remove mountains, but have not love, I am nothing. And though I bestow all my goods to feed *the poor*, and though I give my body to be burned, but have not love, it profits me nothing."

Gifts without grace
You may have the most gifts, or you may have the best gifts,

40

or you may have certain gifts to the highest degree, but if you have not love, you are nothing! Why is love so important? The reason is that this love comes only to those who are converted, who are in Christ. The original Greek word is "agape", which is the special love that only true believers have. An unconverted man may have a lot of compassion, a lot of kindness and so many other things, which together make it appear that they too have this "agape", but that is never the case. It is simply impossible for an unconverted man to have Christian love. Christian love arises only from faith in Jesus Christ. It is found only in converted people, whether in a small measure or in great. The apostle Paul is emphasising the importance of this love in order to stir up the Christians to show more of it.

We must note that it is possible for some people who are not converted to have great gifts. They may profess to be Christians, but they do not truly belong to Christ. That is why the Lord says in Matthew 7:21-23, "Not everyone who says to Me, 'Lord, Lord,' shall enter the kingdom of heaven, but he who does the will of My Father in heaven. Many will say to Me in that day, 'Lord, Lord, have we not prophesied in Your name, cast out demons in Your name, and done many wonders in Your name?' And then I will declare to them, 'I never knew you; depart from Me, you who practise lawlessness!'" Now clearly these are unconverted people. We know from the Bible that whoever comes to Jesus Christ in true faith will not be cast away (John 6:37). It follows that those who have performed so many wondrous things in the name of Christ and yet are cast away, cannot have been truly converted.

You see now why Christian love, "agape", is so important. Without this love, all the gifts you have will amount to nothing!

3.2   Love Behaves In A Certain Way (13:4-7)

Paul moves on to show that this love behaves in a certain way. He says, in verses 4-7, "Love suffers long *and* is kind; love does not envy; love does not parade itself, is not puffed up; does not behave rudely, does not seek its own, is not provoked, thinks no evil; does not rejoice in iniquity, but rejoices in the truth; bears all things, believes all things, hopes all things, endures all things." There is no need for us to analyse every word that is used here to describe love. It is clear that the love that we are talking about is totally selfless; it is totally self-denying; and it is totally self-sacrificing. It is always outward-looking, seeking the good of others. This was what Paul had been advocating earlier in Chapter 12, when he described the church as a body with many parts. He urged that there should be love and unity between the members of the church. Instead of thinking of their own good, instead of competing with one another, instead of engaging in proud and envious rivalry, they should be thinking of the good of others in the church. This was something not seen in the Corinthian church.

Christ our example
We note that the words of verses 4 to 7 are actually the description of Christ Himself. The Lord Jesus Christ is, ultimately speaking, our greatest model of love. You remember how, in John Chapter 13, He washed the disciples' feet and then told them that He had set an example for them to follow. Then, in John 15:12-13, He says, "This is My commandment, that you love one another as I have loved you. Greater love has no one than this, than to lay down one's life for his friends." In 1 Corinthians 11:1 Paul says that we are to imitate him just as he imitated Christ. Christ is therefore our ultimate model. And love is the chief characteristic of Christ.

This love is not to be confused with sentimentality. A lot of people today have a wrong idea of what love is all about. They think that to have this love is to go around with a "holy-dreamy-look", to talk softly, and to tread on tip-toe. But true Christian love is manly, mature, bold, and courageous. Remember how the Lord Jesus Christ overturned the tables of the money-changers in the temple, how He made a cord of whip and drove the animals out of the temple area. Remember how He rebuked the Pharisees and called them "vipers" and "hypocrites". To many Christians today, such behaviour would be regarded as lacking love. But we know better! Christ has shown that true love will speak out against falsehood and errors. True love will expose hypocrisy and heresy in the church.

Similarly, true love will act in a very definite way towards those who are weak, who are seeking to know the Lord and who are lost. Remember how the small-sized Zacchaeus was singled out from the crowd by the Lord, and how he was blessed with the privilege of having the Lord as guest. And we are told that Zacchaeus was saved that day. That was love in action! Clearly, love is not sentimentality. The sentimental emotionalism that passes for love in many churches today is not the type of love that the Lord showed. It is not the love that our present passage is talking about. Paul wants us to know that true Christian love behaves in a certain way. It is selfless, self-denying and self-sacrificing. It is always outward-looking and thinking of the good of other people.

3.3   Love Is Permanent (13:8-13)

We come now to the crucial part of the present chapter. Remember that Paul is teaching us the truth that love is the more excellent way. He argues out his case by first showing to us that love is indispensable. Next, he shows us that love is unique – it behaves in a certain way. He now wants to show us that love is permanent. He says, in verse 8, "Love never fails. But whether *there are* prophecies, they will fail; whether *there are* tongues, they will cease; whether *there is* knowledge, it will vanish away."

Love is a Christian grace. It is something that should characterise a true disciple of Christ. This grace is compared to three gifts which, we are told, will disappear. The three gifts are all revelatory ones. In other words, they are gifts that conveyed the revelation of God to men. A person who spoke in an unknown tongue, that is in a language not previously learned, did so with the idea of revealing God's truth to those who were listening. A person who prophesied uttered words that conveyed God's will to men. A person who had special knowledge was able to inform others of what were normally hidden from the mind of men. Agabus, for example, was able to know that Paul would be arrested in Jerusalem. Peter, for example, was able to know that Ananias and Sapphira were telling a lie. This knowledge is a special gift and not a reference to what we commonly know. Common knowledge will still be in us even when we are in heaven. In heaven, we will know God, we will know one another, we will know truths still.

Love will continue on
Verse 8 tells us that love will continue on while the revelatory gifts will pass away. The contrast stands out more clearly in the original Greek than in the English translation. In the various English translations of the Bible, an attempt has been made to maintain a certain elegance in the prose. This is of course perfectly legitimate, but it loses some of the force of the contrast. We are told that "love never fails". The word "to fail" literally means "to fall". Unlike a fruit that falls from the branch, love never falls. It remains.

A different word is used to describe what would happen to prophecies and knowledge – they "will be abolished", or "will be done away". The word is in the future middle tense, which is very much like the future passive tense. There is here the idea that prophecies and knowledge had only a temporary use, a fact somewhat obscured in the English translation. Prophecies and knowledge were to be rendered of no effect once that temporary use was fulfilled. As for tongues, we are told that they "will cease", or "will come to an end". The word is in the simple future tense. The ability to speak languages that have not been previously learned will naturally cease, or disappear on its own.

We must note that there is no indication that these gifts will be revived once they have ceased. An illustration will be helpful here. Suppose that we visit a man in hospital. We are told by the doctor, "He will die." This is in the simple future tense, in the same way that we are told that tongues "will cease". When the man dies, we would not expect him to be revived. The words used, and the tense employed, do not give any indication at all that he will live again once he had died. Instead of saying, "He will die," the doctor may say, "He will be dead." This is in the passive tense. When the person is actually dead, we do not expect him to become alive again. So also with prophecies and knowledge – when they have been abolished, we do not expect them to be revived. The words and the tense employed do not give any indication that they will be revived. The Charismatics are wrong to claim that tongues, prophecies and knowledge are being revived today. They cannot base their claim on this passage of Scripture. They will have to find some other parts of the Bible to support their claim. They can try, but they will not be able to find any passage that supports that claim!

Which will disappear first? Will it be prophecies? Will it be tongues? Will it be knowledge? This we are not told. The way they are mentioned together, and placed in contrast to love, show that they will disappear at roughly the same time. If they do not all disappear together at exactly the same time, they will disappear close to one another. The basic point made by the apostle is that love will continue on while the revelatory gifts will cease at some time in the future. Love is the more excellent way because it is permanent, while the revelatory gifts are not.

When will the gifts disappear?
Of interest to us is when the revelatory gifts will disappear. We know that it will be at some time after the apostle Paul wrote these words. But when exactly will that time be? Can we know more precisely when that will take place? The subsequent verses show when.

Remember that in this chapter, Paul is trying to show us the more excellent way, which is the way of love. Since he has begun comparing love with the revelatory gifts in verse 8, he continues to talk about them before coming back to talk about love. In the original Greek, verses 9 and 10 actually constitute one sentence, separated only by a semi-colon. Our English Bible translates it into two sentences, which is unfortunate. However, even in the English Bible, we can see quite clearly that the thoughts expressed in the two verses are actually related.

It says in verses 9 and 10, "For we know in part and we prophesy in part. But when that which is perfect has come, then that which is in part will be done away." Many Charismatics would claim, in a rather simplistic way, that the "perfect" in verse 10 refers to heaven or to Christ. The more careful Charismatics would say that the "perfect" refers to the *state* or *condition* in heaven, where we will see Christ "face to face" (verse 12). The "perfect" of verse 10 is thus linked to the "face to face" in verse 12. The comparison made in verses 9 and 10 is, therefore, the imperfect state on earth and the perfect state in heaven. All this sounds so plausible, but we will show that this cannot be right by a careful examination of verses 9 and 10, by a consideration of the context, and from what is said in verse 13. For the moment, we wish to show that the simplistic claim of the vast majority of charismatics, that the "perfect" of verse 10 refers to heaven or Christ, cannot be right. Their basic argument is that prophecy will continue until Christ comes again to earth, or until we arrive in heaven. This is a piecemeal way of interpretation that fails to consider the two verses together as one sentence.

When the two verses are taken together as one sentence, we notice that a comparison is being made between that which is partial and that which is perfect. A comparison is possible only within the same basic realm. For example, I may say to you, "A cow is big, and a cat is small." That sentence will make perfect sense to you because we are comparing one animal with another, and we are talking about their sizes. However, if I were to say to you, "A cow is big, and water is wet," you will think that I am mad! That is because a cow is basically different from water, and size and wetness are totally different qualities. Similarly, in verses 9 and 10, a comparison is being made within the same realm. It is impossible to say that "the perfect" is a reference to Christ or to heaven. If we take "the perfect" to mean Christ or heaven, then "the partial" will have to be a partial Christ or a partial heaven!

In fact, we can see that, in verse 9 and 10, the comparison is between two stages of the same matter. It is like saying, "The cow is small now, but it will be big in a year's time." Paul is saying that what is partial at the time of writing will one day become complete. That is precisely how the word "perfect" is to be understood. In Greek, the word *to teleion* is a neuter word which carries the meaning "the completed thing". It is derived from the word *teleios* which signifies having reached its end, finished, complete. The word is used a total of eighteen times in the New Testament, including this occasion in 1 Corinthians 13:10. Never once is the word used to refer to heaven. And never is it ever used to refer to Christ. Grammatically speaking, it is not possible for masculine words like "heaven" and "Christ" to be qualified by a neuter adjective such as "the perfect".[1]

We have still not stated exactly what "the partial" and "the perfect" mean. We have only noted that it is impossible to

---

[1]Adjectives, like the article, must agree with the nouns which they qualify in number, gender and case.

In 1 Corinthians 13:10, *to teleion* ("the perfect") is actually what is known as a pronominal adjective, i.e. an adjective used in the place of a noun. An example of such an adjective is found in 1 Corinthians 6:9, "Do you not know that the unrighteous will not inherit the kingdom of God?" The word "unrighteous" is an adjective, leading us to ask, "Unrighteous what?" The answer is, of course, unrighteous people! The word "people" is masculine in gender, and so is the pronominal adjective "the unrighteous". In 1 Corinthians 13:10, "the perfect" is a *neuter* pronominal adjective. How can a *neuter* adjective be used to qualify *masculine* nouns like "Christ" or "heaven"?

Of course, it is possible for a neuter adjective to describe a neuter quality *of Christ* or *of heaven*. In Romans 1:19, "*what may be known* of God" is neuter, and so is "*the invisible things (attributes) of Him*" in Romans 1:20. These examples are fairly straightforward since the "of God" and "of Him" are given. If this is intended in 1 Corinthians 13:10, why didn't the apostle just add "of Christ" or "of heaven"?

Furthermore, the argument from the gender of the word should not obscure the fact that verse 10 should be interpreted in conjunction with verse 9, and also in the light of the context of the passage.

equate the "perfect" with Christ or heaven. Since verses 9 and 10 together form one sentence, and a comparison is obviously being made between them, we should put them side by side:

> Verse 9 says, "For we know in part and we prophesy in part;"
>
> Verse 10 says, "but when that which is perfect has come, then that which is in part will be done away."

We have noted that when a person prophesies, he is actually revealing God's will to men. Verse 9 is saying that our prophecy is partial, or incomplete, because our knowledge of God's will is partial or incomplete. Since what "we know in part" in verse 9 is the revelation of God, "that which is perfect" in verse 10 must be the complete revelation of God. It is significant that while the word "perfect" is never used of Christ or heaven, it is used of Scriptures in James 1:25, which says, "But he who looks into the perfect law of liberty and continues in it, and is not a forgetful hearer but a doer of the work, this one will be blessed in what he does."

Next, we compare the second part of verse 10 with the second part of verse 9. The "that which is in part" of verse 10 must be a reference to the prophesying of verse 9. Prophecy was only a temporary vehicle for transmitting God's will to men at the time when the revelation of God was not yet completely given. When the revelation of God is completely given, then prophecy "will be done away". The word translated "will be done away" in verse 10 is exactly the same word used in verse 8 about prophecies and knowledge, which "will be done away", or "abolished".

One dictionary of New Testament words (Vine's) actually says that in 1 Corinthians 13:10, the word "perfect" refers to "the complete revelation of God's will and ways, whether in the completed Scriptures or in the hereafter." Here, we have at least a confirmation that the "perfect" of verse 10 cannot be a reference to Christ or heaven but rather, it is "the complete revelation of God's will and ways". We have still to determine when that will happen. Will it happen with the completion of

Scriptures or will it happen in heaven? The context will give us the answer.

When revelation will be complete
If Paul is referring to heaven, when the revelation of God will be complete, the contrast between love and the revelatory gifts in verse 8 will not stand out too clearly. Love is supposed to be the more excellent way because it lasts longer than the gifts. Also, it would fail to take into consideration the unique phenomenon of Scriptures. Put another way, it would mean that the Bible is not the unique revelation of God since there are these other means of revelation, namely prophecies, tongues and knowledge. The sole authority of the Bible, in all matters of doctrine and practice, would then be undermined. A third difficulty will arise from that. If the written word of God is not unique, and the revelatory gifts continue today, then we may add new prophecies to the Bible. Furthermore, the comparison made between love and the two other graces, namely faith and hope, in verse 13, will not be possible. These are formidable problems, which will not be encountered if we adopt a different view.

At the time when Paul was writing 1 Corinthians, the revelation of God was still not completely written down. All the apostles of Christ knew that they were actually writing the revelation of God. We read in 2 Peter 3:15-16 these words, "...as also our beloved brother Paul, according to the wisdom given to him, has written to you, as also in all his epistles, speaking in them of these things, in which are some things hard to understand, which untaught and unstable *people* twist to their own destruction, as *they do* also the rest of the Scriptures." Peter said that untaught and unstable people were twisting the words of Paul just as they were twisting *the rest of the Scriptures*. Clearly, Peter recognized that what the apostle Paul had written down were Scriptures. We can be sure that the other apostles were aware of the fact that they were writing Scriptures as well.

The Scriptures were completed once the last surviving apostle, John, wrote the book of Revelation. It is significant that he ended that book by warning us not to add to, or subtract from, the prophecy of the book (Revelation 22:18-19). Since that is the last book of Scripture, we expect no more revelation to be given after that. There were no more prophets and apostles after the time of John. The church on earth is being "built on the foundation of the apostles and prophets, Jesus Christ Himself being the chief cornerstone" (Ephesians 2:20). The phrase "the apostles and prophets" means, of course, their writings, which point us to Christ.

We read in 2 Timothy 3:16-17 these words, "All Scripture is given by inspiration of God, and is profitable for doctrine, for reproof, for correction, for instruction in righteousness, that the man of God may be complete, thoroughly equipped for every good work." This was written by the apostle Paul, who knew that the Scriptures would be all that a man needs to guide him into a knowledge of God's will. When we consider what he wrote in 1 Corinthians 13 in the light of this passage, we become aware that Paul was looking forward to the time when the Scriptures would be completely written.

We conclude, therefore, that "the perfect" of 1 Corinthians 13:10 is a reference to the complete revelation of God as contained in the Bible, and "that which is in part" which will be done away is prophesying, and the associated gifts of tongues and knowledge. The prophecies, tongues and knowledge mentioned in verse 8, which were expected to vanish away with the completion of the revelation of God, are therefore not found anymore today.

A child growing up
In verse 11 to 12, two illustrations are used by the apostle to emphasise the temporary nature of prophecies, tongues and knowledge. The first illustration is that of a child growing to maturity. The speech of a child is "childish" since his understanding has not developed. A baby would learn to utter sounds such as "Ma ma", or "Pa pa", without knowing what those sounds mean. As he grows, he begins to associate those

sounds with summoning people and getting their attention. When he sees a man visiting the home, he might call the person "Papa" without realising that he is not his father! Soon, he learns to call only his mother and father "Mama" and "Papa", and there would be no more embarrassment caused!

As the child grows, he begins to repeat words after the mother to form complete sentences. When he is older, he forms his own sentences without the aid of the mother. When he matures further, he begins to express his thoughts with words of his own. By this stage, the child has already grown up! He would no longer be uttering unintelligible sounds. He would no longer be uttering sentences after others which make no sense to him. He would be thinking and behaving as an adult. It says, in verse 11, "When I was a child, I spoke as a child, I understood as a child, I thought as a child; but when I became a man, I put away childish things."

Note that, in this verse, what is spoken, understood, and thought of, all have to do with what we know. This verse is, in fact, an illustration of our understanding of God's revelation. It is incomplete at first, and becomes more and more complete with time, so that a stage comes when childish ways are put aside. The church had to rely on the childish methods of prophecies, tongues and knowledge to know the will of God before the Scriptures were completely given. Once the revelation of God was completely given, these childish ways were stopped.

Looking into a mirror
The next illustration is that of a person looking into the mirror. It says in verse 12, "For now we see in a mirror, dimly, but then face to face." The Charismatics often appeal to this verse to support their claim that the revelatory gifts continue today and will only cease in heaven. They say that the "face to face" means seeing Jesus Christ in person, linking this with verse 10 in which it is claimed that the "perfect" is a reference to Christ or heaven. We have already seen that the "perfect" of verse 10 cannot be a reference to Christ or heaven. But what does "face

to face" in verse 12 mean? Literally, it means to see a person directly. This phrase, however, is not always used literally in the Bible.

In Exodus 33:11, for example, we are told that "the LORD spoke to Moses face to face, as a man speaks to his friend." It is obvious that the phrase "face to face" cannot be taken literally here because God is a spirit and has no form. Furthermore, if a man were to see God, he would be struck dead by His glory. We are told in verse 20 of that chapter that God said to Moses, "You cannot see My face; for no man shall see Me, and live." We are told further that God would put Moses in the cleft of a rock while His glory passed by, and, verse 23, "Then I will take away My hand, and you shall see My back; but My face shall not be seen."

If the phrase, "face to face" cannot be taken literally, what does it actually mean? The answer may be found in Numbers 12:5-9. We are told in verse 5, "Then the LORD came down in a pillar of cloud and stood in the door of the tabernacle, and called Aaron and Miriam." Verse 9 says, "So the anger of the LORD was aroused against them, and He departed." This was a *theophany* – a manifestation of God in the form of a man.

We look next at verses 6 to 8, which say, "Then He said, 'Hear now My words: if there is a prophet among you, *I*, the LORD, make Myself known to him in a vision; I speak to him in a dream. Not so with My servant Moses; he is faithful in all My house. I speak with him face to face, even plainly, and not in dark sayings; and he sees the form of the LORD. Why then were you not afraid to speak against My servant Moses?'" Here, the emphasis is on God revealing Himself to Moses in a special way. The emphasis is not with the mere encounter with the person of God. Aaron and Miriam literally saw the form of God, just as Moses did. Moses was singled out as different from Aaron and Miriam, and from other prophets. He was specially treated with being given a fuller and clearer revelation of God.

The meaning of "face to face" is obvious from the passage. It means "plainly, clearly, or fully". The revelation which Moses received from God was given directly, and was more complete, as compared with the other prophets. Note two things about this passage: firstly, the comparison is between two types of revelation, both of which were infallible, but one of which was more complete and clearer; and, secondly, the "face to face" experience took place on earth, and not in heaven.[2]

It is wrong of the Charismatics to claim a "secondary prophecy" which is a mixture of truth and error. All prophecies that came from God were always true. A person whose prophecy contained any element of falsehood would have been treated as a false prophet, and he would have been stoned to death. This is according to the teaching of Deuteronomy 18:20-22, "But the prophet who presumes to speak a word in My name, which I have not commanded him to speak, or who speaks in the name of other gods, that prophet shall die. And if you say in your heart, 'How shall we know the word which the LORD has not spoken?' – when a prophet speaks in the name of the LORD, if the thing does not happen or come to pass, that is the thing which the LORD has not spoken; the prophet has spoken it presumptuously; you shall not be afraid of him." Today, we find many Charismatics uttering prophecies that prove to be false. What they claim is not in accordance with Scripture, and what they predict does not come true. Yet nothing is done about them! In the Old Testament time, they would have been stoned to death! Today, church discipline should at least be exercised upon them. But that has not been done, and these people are allowed to continue uttering their so-called "prophecies"!

---

[2]It is to be noted that the expression "face to face" in Numbers 12:8 is literally "mouth to mouth" in the original language, emphasising that revelation is referred to throughout, not the visual perception of God. The Bible translators have been right in recognising that the expression "mouth to mouth" is equivalent to "face to face", both in the Old and New Testaments (2 John 12; 3 John 14). Moses is singled out as specially favoured by God in Exodus 33:11 and Deuteronomy 34:10 just as in Numbers 12:8, except that in, these other passages, the expression used in the original language is "face to face" and not "mouth to mouth". Clearly, the two expressions are equivalent, and clearly they are a reference to the revelation of God and not to a literal visual, perception of God.

We come back to 1 Corinthians 13:12, "For now we see in a mirror, dimly, but then face to face." We must understand that at the time when Paul wrote these words, the mirrors were made of polished metals. They were not made of mercury-coated glass like what we have today. When a person looked into the mirror of those days, he could only see his own image dimly. This is to illustrate the truth that the believers during Paul's time could know the will of God only incompletely because the revelation of God had not been completely given. We must also remember that Paul was trained as a rabbi, and he knew the Old Testament Scriptures very well. He often used Old Testament expressions and imagery in his writings. Here, Paul was expecting the revelation of God to be completed some time in the future, when a believer would know God "face to face", just as Moses knew God face to face.

1 Corinthians 13:12 goes on to say, "Now I know in part, but then I shall know just as I also am known." Instead of treating this as a new illustration, it seems best to take it as an elaboration of the earlier part, "For now we see in a mirror, dimly, but then face to face." This is for the reason that, in the original Greek, the two parts constitute one sentence, separated by a semi-colon. Placing the two parts of the one sentence side by side, we have:

> For now we see in a mirror, dimly, but then face to face;
>
> now I know in part, but then I shall know just as I also am known.

As in verses 9 and 10, we must compare the second part of the sentence with the first part. The phrase "now I know in part" must correspond with "now we see in a mirror, dimly". It must mean that our knowledge of God's will is partial or incomplete.

The phrase, "but then I shall know as I also am known" must correspond with "but then face to face". This means that our knowledge of God will become complete, instead of remaining partial. It is as though we see someone's reflection in the mirror dimly, while he sees us clearly. As we turn around, we see him clearly just as we are clearly seen by him. Here, the "face to face" experience is with God, and in a figurative sense, with reference to His revelation. Earlier, we have referred to Exodus 33:11, which says, "So the LORD spoke to Moses face to face, as a man speaks to his friend." In the next two verses, Moses said to the Lord, "See, You say to me, 'Bring up this people.' But You have not let me know whom You will send with me. Yet You have said, 'I know you by name, and you have also found grace in My sight.' Now therefore, I pray, if I have found grace in Your sight, show me now Your way, that I may know You and that I may find grace in Your sight, and consider that this nation is Your people." Here, we are told that Moses desired to know the Lord by knowing His way. To know God's way is to know Him. Moses desired to know God as he was known by God.

We are known by God fully and clearly, whereas our knowledge of God is partial. In a sense, it will always be partial, even when we arrive in heaven. Being creatures, we will never be able to know the infinite God completely. In 1 Corinthians 13:12, however, Paul has the specific purpose of comparing the situation at the time of writing with the situation at a time in the future. His purpose was to show that the revelatory gifts would pass away when the revelation of God became complete.

We have earlier noted that the word "perfect" is used to describe the law of God in James 1:25, "But he who looks into the perfect law of liberty and continues *in it*, and is not a forgetful hearer but a doer of the work, this one will be blessed in what he does." It is of interest to note that, on this occasion, James is actually referring to the law of God as a mirror. He says, in verses 22 to 23, "For if anyone is a hearer of the word and not a doer, he is like a man observing his natural face in a mirror; for he observes himself, goes away, and immediately forgets what kind of man he was." The early Christians looked upon the law of God as a mirror that showed them what they were like. While their literal mirror could only show their images dimly, the perfect law of God could show them their true selves, just as God saw them. The law of God reveals to us the ugliness of our sins. It shows us that our righteousness is nothing but filthy rags before God. It reveals to us the Lord Jesus Christ, and how redemption is to be found in Him alone.

Love is the greatest
Let us stand back and consider the whole passage again. In verse 8, we are told that the revelatory gifts will pass away. We wish to determine when that would happen. Verses 9 and 10 show us that it will happen when the revelation of God has been completely given. Two illustrations follow, both of which clearly speak of the revelation of God, which will become complete. There is the illustration of the child growing to maturity, in verse 11. Then there is the illustration of seeing into the mirror dimly, which would give way to seeing "face to face". We may now draw the clear conclusion that the revelatory gifts would pass away when the Bible was completely written. Once that happened, there would have been no purpose left for the revelatory gifts.

Confirmation of this conclusion is found in verse 13, "And now abide faith, hope, love, these three; but the greatest of these is love." The definition of faith is given in Hebrews 11:1, "Now faith is the substance of things hoped for, the evidence of things not seen." Romans 8:24-25 explains to us what is hope, "For we were saved in this hope, but hope that is seen is not hope; for why does one still hope for what he sees? But if we hope for what we do not see, we eagerly wait for it with perseverance." This is how "faith" and "hope" are to be understood. When we arrive in heaven, there would be no more need for faith and hope. Only love remains. For that reason, love is the greatest of the three graces.

We have noted earlier the difficulties that would be faced if we say that the revelatory gifts will cease only at the second coming of Christ. If that is the case, we would have to take it that faith, hope and love will continue in heaven. We would then need to redefine faith and hope. We would also have to find a reason why it is that love is the greatest of the three.

By holding to the interpretation that we have given, all these difficulties will not arise. Instead, there will be consistency in the arguments of the chapter. Love is the more excellent way because: (i) it is indispensable, (ii) it is unique, and (iii) it is permanent. Concerning the permanency of love, it never fails while the revelatory gifts will cease with the completion of Scriptures. Graces are greater than the revelatory gifts because they will remain when the latter have passed away. Of the three graces, love is greatest because it lasts to eternity, while faith and hope ends with the second coming of Christ.[3]

The authority of Scripture
We know from the history of the church that prophecies and knowledge stopped, and tongues gradually faded away, at the completion of the Bible.[4] That was why the early ecumenical councils were held whenever the church was threatened by heresies. These councils must not be confused with the ecumenical movement of today. In those days, the church leaders would meet to discuss any heresy that had arisen. They would then issue a decree to condemn the heresy and declare what they believed to be the teaching of the Bible. The early Christians did not resort to prophecies, tongues or knowledge to determine the will of God. Instead, they treated the word of God as complete and sufficient. They used it as the authoritative rule to determine what were true and what were false.

The early Christians knew very well that the words of Revelation 22:18-21 closed the revelation of God. The completed

---

[3]The question is often raised, Is it not possible that this passage is referring to heaven as well as to the completion of Scripture? We would not exclude the thought of heaven, for all the teachings of Scripture are intended to prepare us for heaven. After all, we have seen that love will continue on in heaven (1 Corinthians 13:13). However, we should not hesitate to say that the *immediate* reference of the passage is to the completion of Scripture.

[4]No significant group is known to have claimed the gifts in the first fifty years after the completion of the Bible. Various extreme groups arose later which claimed the restoration of the gifts but there was no continuity between them. These sporadic groups were never significant, whether compared to "mainline Christianity" or "dissenting Christianity".

Scriptures will be all that is needed until Christ comes again. Verses 18 and 19 say, "For I testify to everyone who hears the words of the prophecy of this book: If anyone adds to these things, God will add to him the plagues that are written in this book; and if anyone takes away from the words of the book of this prophecy, God shall take away his part from the Book of Life, from the holy city, and from the things which are written in this book." The "adding to" and "taking away from" must not be restricted to the written words of the Bible only, but to its teaching as well. The Charismatics today claim that they utter "secondary prophecies" which, although not on par with Scriptures, are prophecies from God. They claim that these "secondary prophecies", which may be mixed with error, are not added to the Bible as Scriptures. We have seen that it is not possible to have true prophecies that are mixed with error. We must point out now that to claim prophecies today is to "add to" the teaching of the Bible, and to fail to uphold the completion and sufficiency of Scriptures is to "take away from" the teaching God's word. It is to break the command given in Revelation 22:18-19. We should be expounding the word of God today, and not be engaging in tongue-speaking and prophecy. Expounding the word of God is different from claiming fresh revelation from God.

3.4   Conclusion

We have shown where the Charismatics are wrong in their interpretation of certain verses in 1 Corinthians 13. They have the tendency to adopt a piecemeal approach in the interpretation of Scriptures, and fail to look at the verses in their proper contexts. This has resulted in fantastic claims being made by them. One such claim is that there is a necessary connection between the spirituality of a Christian and the gifts he possesses. If the claim is not made explicitly, it is assumed. Go to any Charismatic circle, and you will soon get the idea that one has to speak in tongues to be a better Christian! Stay with them for a while, and you will find that prophecies and special knowledge are claimed freely! The chief characteristic of the Charismatic movement is the free exercise of the tongues, prophecies, and healing, with claims of knowledge and visions. Our study of 1 Corinthians 13 has shown that: (i) there is no necessary connection between spirituality and gifts; and (ii) the revelatory gifts of prophecies, tongues and knowledge have ceased. A person can have the greatest, and most gifts, but he may be devoid of Christian love. The revelation of God is complete, and the Bible alone is the only authority in all matters of faith and practice.

We close with one more point: the completion of Scriptures is taught in the context of the indispensability of love, together with a description of how that love behaves. Christian love and Bible knowledge are married together. To love Christ is to obey His commandments (John 14:15). Without knowing the teaching of the Bible, it is impossible to love God truly. Equally, all our knowledge of the Bible's teaching amounts to nothing if we do not show love to others. After all, loving God involves also loving our neighbours as ourselves! Love and truth are inseparable. If you claim to have truth, do you show forth love?

Four

PROPHECY IS GREATER THAN TONGUES (1 Corinthians 14:1-25)

We have been studying spiritual gifts. Chapters 12 to 14 of 1 Corinthians provide the most extensive teaching on this subject in the Bible. In 1 Corinthians 12, the apostle Paul showed us that the church is one body. Nothing sinful or selfish should be done to break the unity of the body of Christ. In that chapter, we learned also that there are different types of gifts from God to His people. Some gifts are greater than others, and we are to desire the greater gifts (1 Corinthians 12:31). The apostle ended the chapter by saying. "And yet I show you a more excellent way."

What is that more excellent way? He showed us, in Chapter 13, that the more excellent way is the way of love. Love is the more excellent way because it is indispensable, it is unique, and it lasts forever. We have learned from that chapter that graces are more important than gifts. Put another way, Christian character is more important than all our abilities. Three graces were singled out for mention, namely faith, hope, and love. These were contrasted with the revelatory gifts of prophecies, tongues and knowledge. The revelatory gifts ceased with the completion of the revelation of God in the Bible. Of the graces, love is the greatest since it will last to eternity, while faith and hope will disappear at the second coming of Christ.

4.1   Preliminary Considerations

Healings and miracles uncommon
In Chapter 14, the apostle leads us back to the topic of the spiritual gifts. He singles out prophecy and tongues for comparison. It is significant that he does not mention the gifts of healings and miracles in this chapter. Miracles and healings were listed among the gifts in 1 Corinthians 12:28, but they are not mentioned at all in Chapter 14. Charismatics often give the impression that healings and miracles were common occurrences among the Christians of the New Testament time. The Bible, however, does not teach that this was the case. In fact, we are told that only a small circle of people had the gifts of healings and miracles. We will have occasion to come back to this. At the moment, we wish only to point out that healings and miracles were not widely practised by the Christians of the New Testament time. These were the marks of the apostles (2 Corinthians 12:12). The problem in Corinth was not so much that people were performing healings and miracles. Rather, the problem was the exercise of the gifts of prophecy and tongues, and especially tongues.

The Corinthian church appeared to be agitated over these two gifts, and especially over that of tongues. When people spoke in foreign languages which they had not previously learned, there was that aura of mysticism involved. The dramatic element was more obvious. It was clearly a supernatural gift. When others uttered a prophecy, the drama was not there. A prophecy was uttered in a language known to the hearers. There was that difference between the two gifts. It is therefore easy to understand why there was so much attention given to tongue-speaking. It attracted the attention of the less stable. It distracted those who were not clear about the purpose of coming together to worship. In this chapter, Paul wishes to show that prophecy is in fact better than tongues. In so doing, he will be laying down some important principles of worship, and of how the gifts are to be used.

What are prophecy and tongues?
What was prophecy? And what were tongues? We have seen in our previous study that a prophecy was the inspired utterance of a man which conveyed the will of God to other people. It was the telling forth of God's revelation, which could include the events that God intended to bring to pass. A prophecy was therefore not just "foretelling", but also "forthtelling". It was, by definition, infallible. Inspired revelation from God could not possibly turn out to be false. We are told in 2 Peter 1:21 that "prophecy never came by the will of man, but holy men of God spoke *as they were* moved by the Holy Spirit." In the Old Testament time, those whose prophecy turned out to be false had to be stoned to death (Deuteronomy 18:20-22).

It should be noted that a gift may be possessed by a person who occupies an office as well as by others who do not occupy any office. Those who are called by God to be pastors should preach the word since that is the duty belonging to their office. However, other Christians who are not pastors may also be gifted with the ability to preach. They should preach the word whenever there is the opportunity to do so. The same may be said of prophecy. There were prophets in the New Testament time. Their job was to convey the revelation of God to men. Others, however, were, also occasionally given the ability to prophesy. In Acts 21:9, for example, we are told that Philip, the evangelist, had four daughters who prophesied. We are not told that they were prophetesses, in the same sense that Agabus was a prophet (Acts 21:10). Similarly, we are told in 1 Corinthians 11:4 and 5 that there were men and women who prophesied. This means that they were given the ability to convey the revelation of God to others in the church. Prophecies were the inspired revelation of God given to certain people, whether or not they were prophets.

What about the gift of tongues? This was actually the ability to speak in human languages, not previously learned, which conveyed God's revelation to men. In Acts 2:4, we are told that the early disciples were filled with the Holy Spirit and began to speak with other tongues. What were these tongues? We are told in the subsequent verses that these were the languages of the people who lived around the Mediterranean region. The same Greek word, *glossa*, is used in Acts 2 and in 1 Corinthians. The word is translated "tongues", meaning "languages". When we ask someone, "What is your mother-tongue?", we are actually trying to find out what language he speaks at home. Today, the word "tongues" is hardly used in everyday conversation. This has caused a lot of people to think that the "tongues" mentioned in the Bible were some unknown and extraordinary utterances. In the Indonesian Bible (the *Alkitab*), the word in 1 Corinthians is translated as "*bahasa roh*" which means "spiritual languages", or "languages of the spirit". In the Malay Bible (the *Alkitab Berita Baik*), the word is translated as "*bahasa yang ajaib*" which means "miraculous languages". These translations are obviously wrong. The word should have been translated in the same way as in Acts 2, *bahasa lain*, i.e. "other languages". The wrong translations have reinforced the wrong assumptions of the Charismatics that tongues are unintelligible sounds which come from the Holy Spirit. No, tongues were human languages! This must be kept in mind as we study 1 Corinthians 14. Otherwise, you will face difficulties in understanding this portion of Scripture.

4.2 Prophecy Edifies The Church (14:1-5)

The first point made by the apostle is that prophecy is greater than tongues because it edifies the church. He had just concluded the digression on love. He now says, in verse 1, "Pursue love, and desire spiritual *gifts*, but especially that you may prophesy." So far, in his discussion on the gifts, Paul appeared to have been rather negative and unenthusiastic about the Corinthian claims to the gifts. He might easily be misunderstood as wanting his readers to forget about the gifts altogether and, instead, to pursue love and unity in the church. This is where Paul corrects this possible misunderstanding concerning his view on the matter.

He tells his readers to pursue love, since love is so important. Love needs to be pursued, or followed after. The word "pursue" may be translated as "to press forward", or "to make progress in". Effort is needed to have more and more of this love. Love needs to be shown in increasing measure. Graces are different from gifts. Graces, such as faith, hope and love, are given to all Christians in different measures. Gifts, on the other hand, are given only according to God's sovereign will. Everyone has a gift from God, but not everyone has all the gifts. It may be that you desire to have certain gifts, but it is up to God to distribute them to you. We may desire the greater gifts, but we must never demand that God give them to us. Gifts are only to be desired, or coveted, while graces must be pursued. Of course, gifts that are already given to you should be "pursued" as well, i.e. we are to make progress in them. Gifts you do not have may be desired but not demanded. We see Paul making this point about gifts all the time. In 1 Corinthians 12:31, he said, "But earnestly desire the best gifts." In 1 Corinthians 14:39, he tells the readers to "earnestly desire to prophesy".

Why is prophecy to be desired more than tongues? Paul says in verse 2, "For he who speaks in a tongue does not speak to men but to God, for no one understands *him*; however, in the spirit he speaks mysteries." Before you jump to conclusions of your own, make sure that you seek out the meaning of these words from the Scripture. Speaking in tongues is not the uttering of gibberish. It is not the making of unintelligible sounds. It is the uttering of words that make sense. When a person spoke in a tongue, he would not be understood by others around him. That was because the language was unknown to them. It was nevertheless a human language that conveyed sense to those who could understand. If it were the mere utterance of a string of unintelligible sounds, it would not be considered as being spoken. The verse, however, shows that the tongue was being *spoken*. The person "*speaks* in a tongue", and he "*speaks* to God". This is the first thing to be noted from this verse. Speaking in a tongue is the speaking in a language.

The second thing to be noted is that the speaker knows what he is saying. Others might not understand him because he is speaking in a foreign language, but it is impossible that he himself does not understand what is being uttered. That is what is implied in the word "to speak". He speaks "in the spirit", meaning that he speaks what his inner self knows. The spirit of man does know. It says in Mark 2:8, "But immediately, when Jesus perceived in His spirit that they reasoned thus within themselves, He said to them..." In Luke 1:46-47, we read that Mary burst out in praise, saying, "My soul magnifies the Lord, and my spirit has rejoiced in God my Saviour." In Matthew 26:41, the Lord told His disciples, "Watch and pray, lest you enter into temptation. The spirit indeed *is* willing, but the flesh *is* weak." In all these passages, we see that the spirit is a reference to the inner being of a person. We see also that the spirit of a man is capable of knowing.

Some people might argue that the last phrase of verse 2 should be translated without "the" before "spirit", so that it reads, "in spirit he speaks mysteries". That way, the phrase would sound like John 4:23 and 24 in which the Lord says that those who worship God must worship "in spirit and truth". That cannot be right, however, because the word "in" is not found in 1 Corinthians 14:2 as in the passage in John's gospel. Moreover, comparison with verses 14 to 16 of 1 Corinthians 14 shows that Paul is talking about the spirit of man, for there, the definite article is found before the word "spirit". Of course, we are not excluding the idea that one must pray sincerely, from the heart, "in spirit". We must, however, be more precise in our understanding of Scripture. Paul is referring to the spirit, or soul, of man. We have noted that, in Luke 1:46-47, Mary said, "My soul magnifies the Lord, and my spirit has rejoiced in

God my Saviour." The words "soul" and "spirit" are used interchangeably to refer to the inner being of a person, in contrast to the body. The spirit, of course, expresses itself through the body. What we are pointing out is that the person who speaks in the spirit knows what he is saying. He does not go into a state of ecstasy in which there is no consciousness of what is being uttered.

We note next that the word "mystery" carries a different meaning in the Bible compared with the way it is used in everyday life. Many of us grew up on a diet of Enid Blyton's books which often involve the solving of mysteries. To many people, therefore, the word "mystery" means an unknown, inexplicable and perplexing occurrence. When the case is solved, it ceases to be a mystery. The Bible, however, uses the word in a different way. We read in Romans 16:25-27 these words, "Now to Him who is able to establish you according to my gospel and the preaching of Jesus Christ, according to the revelation of the mystery kept secret since the world began but now made manifest, and by the prophetic Scriptures made known to all nations, according to the commandment of the everlasting God, for obedience to the faith – to God, alone wise, *be* glory through Jesus Christ forever. Amen." Here, the word "mystery" is a reference to the gospel. The gospel is the message about Christ and how men of all nations are to be saved through faith in Him. The saving of all nations was a truth totally unknown to the non-Jews and hidden from the understanding of many Jews. The identity of the Saviour was also unknown to everyone before the time of John the Baptist (John 1:31). All these were now being made known through the apostles. The message of salvation would have remained hidden if not revealed by God. Although made clear now by revelation, it continues to be called a "mystery". A mystery, therefore, is something that would have remained hidden from the knowledge of men if not revealed by God.

The word "mystery" is used in the same way in Ephesians 3:2-6. The passage says, "...you have heard of the dispensation of the grace of God which was given to me for you, how that by revelation He made known to me the mystery (as I have briefly written already, by which, when you read, you may understand my knowledge in the mystery of Christ), which in other ages was not made known to the sons of men, as it has now been revealed by the Spirit to His holy apostles and prophets: that the Gentiles should be fellow heirs, of the same body, and partakers of His promise in Christ through the gospel..." The word is used in the same way again in Colossians 1:25-27, "...I became a minister according to the stewardship from God which was given to me for you, to fulfil the word of God, the mystery which has been hidden from ages and from generations, but now has been revealed to His saints. To them God willed to make known what are the riches of the glory of this mystery among the Gentiles: which is Christ in you, the hope of glory." We see, from all these passages, that "mystery" is not something that is unknown. Rather, it is something that is now made known by God. It is a reference to the revelation of God.

Coming back to 1 Corinthians 14:2, we note that the one who speaks in a tongue is not uttering something unknown. Rather, he is speaking in a human language the things revealed to him by God. The thoughts, or ideas, expressed by that language are known to God and to the speaker.

We take pains to clarify this point because the Charismatics are saying that those who speak in tongues do not know what they are uttering. In fact, they are teaching people to speak in so-called "tongues" by emptying their minds, and letting loose their tongues to produce some sounds, and letting their tongues roll without being hampered by thoughts. This sort of teaching is not found anywhere in the Bible. We do not find a single passage anywhere teaching people how to get the gift of tongues. This teaching is, in fact, contrary to what we know of God's dealings with man. God would never reduce a person to a mere robot, such that he utters words or sounds without understanding. The rational faculty in man is always preserved and respected. The importance of the mind is constantly emphasised in the Bible. We are constantly exhorted to be sober-minded (Romans 12:3; 2 Timothy 1:7; Titus 1:8;

2:6).

The contrast between tongues and prophecy is not yet completed. Paul goes on to say, in verse 3, "But he who prophesies speaks edification and exhortation and comfort to men." People are able to benefit from prophecy simply because they understand what is being spoken. This is clear when taken together with the earlier verse in which Paul said that the no one understands when a person speaks in a tongue.

In verse 4, the apostle says, "He who speaks in a tongue edifies himself, but he who prophesies edifies the church." Why is prophecy greater than tongues? When a person speaks in a tongue, only he himself knows what is said. God may have revealed something to him, which he now utters out by an unknown language. If others in the church do not understand that language, they are not edified. On the other hand, if he makes known the revelation of God in a known language, that is, if he prophesies, others will be edified. For people to be strengthened and built up in the faith, they must hear the word of God with understanding.

The only way tongues can edify others is when they are interpreted. As long as those tongues are not interpreted, people will remain ignorant of what has been said. This is made clear by Paul when he says, in verse 5, "I wish you all spoke with tongues, but even more that you prophesied; for he who prophesies is greater than he who speaks with tongues, unless indeed he interprets, that the church may receive edification."

Paul is not trying to stop anyone from speaking in tongues. At the time of writing, the gifts of tongues and prophecy had not been withdrawn. The Bible had not been completely written. Those gifts were still available to some people. All gifts from God would accomplish some good, tongues included. But Paul would rather that the Corinthian Christians prophesy so that the whole church might be edified. He wants them to stop thinking of themselves, and their own edification only. He does not want them to be selfish and self-centred. He wants them to think of the good of others. The one who is able to edify the church is greater than the one who only edifies himself.

Prophecy is greater than tongues because it edifies the whole church while tongues only edifies the speaker.

4.3 The Understanding Is Important (14:6-19)

Before proceeding to another reason why prophecy is greater than tongues, Paul wishes to spend some time on explaining the importance of the understanding. He does this in two steps. First, he shows that prophesying is immediately understood by the hearers. Then, he shows that tongues must be interpreted so that the hearers may understand.

Prophesying is easily understood
He says, in verse 6, "But now, brethren, if I come to you speaking with tongues, what shall I profit you unless I speak to you either by revelation, by knowledge, by prophesying, or by teaching?" It is possible that, here, Paul is repeating "revelation" and "knowledge" by using as alternatives "prophesying" and "teaching", for emphasis. In prophecy, the revelation of God is imparted to the hearers, and in teaching, the knowledge of God's will is imparted. Whatever the case may be, we should not miss the thrust of the sentence. The main point is that the hearers will be able to profit only when they understand what is being spoken. We may paraphrase the verse like this: "But now, brethren, what will you gain if I speak to you in any language unless you understand what I am saying?"

The importance of the understanding is further stressed by two illustrations. It says, in verse 7, "Even things without life, whether flute or harp, when they make a sound, unless they make a distinction in the sounds, how will it be known what is piped or played?" Musical instruments, like the flute and the harp, are useful only when intelligible sounds are produced. The notes have to be distinct and they must be arranged in sequence, according to certain combinations, so as to produce music. Otherwise, these instruments will merely be churning out useless sounds that irritate the ears. We all know what it is like when a child blows on a harmonica or strikes a piano in a haphazard way. It is certainly not pleasing to the ears! And we would not call that music!

The next illustration is taken from the battlefield. In the old days, battles were fought by the armies of the two opposing parties coming together in battle arrays. They then clashed and fought hand-to-hand combats. The soldiers were summoned to battle stations by the blowing of certain prearranged notes on the trumpet. The apostle Paul asks the rhetorical question, in verse 8, "For if the trumpet makes an uncertain sound, who will prepare for battle?" The obvious answer is, "None!" No one will prepare for battle since the call for battle has not been given clearly. Before anyone will act, he must understand the notes of the trumpet call. The understanding is so important!

Verse 9 says, "So likewise you, unless you utter by the tongue words easy to understand, how will it be known what is spoken? For you will be speaking into the air." The phrase "speaking into the air" means speaking in vain. A similar phrase was used by the apostle in Chapter 9 of this same epistle, in which he said, in verse 26, "Therefore I run thus: not with uncertainty. Thus I fight: not as *one who* beats the air." There, he was using the illustration of the public games to exhort believers to live a disciplined life. A person running in the Olympic games will run with determination. A boxer will ensure that his punches hit the opponent, and not the air. To "beat the air" was to punch in a useless way. To "speak into the air" is to speak uselessly. All your speaking, in whatever language, amounts to nothing if the words are not understood by the hearers.

Verses 10-11 say, "There are, it may be, so many kinds of languages in the world, and none of them is without significance. Therefore, if I do not know the meaning of the language, I shall be a foreigner to him who speaks, and he who speaks *will be* a foreigner to me." The word translated as "foreigner" literally means "barbarian". It is a reference to uncivilised, uncultured people. Civilisation and culture are, of course, relative terms. What is meant here is that the two parties meeting together will be total strangers to each other. What Paul is saying may be paraphrased like this, "All languages in the world do convey ideas. If I do not understand the language spoken, I will be a total stranger to the one speaking and he will be a total stranger to me." We have an expression in Chinese which describes such a situation: the two parties concerned will be "like a chicken and a duck". The chicken may continue saying "Chick! Chick! Chick!", and the duck "Quack! Quack! Quack!", but it will be useless. One cannot understand the other!

Paul now relates the importance of the understanding to the spiritual gifts. He says to them in verse 12, "Even so you, since you are zealous for spiritual *gifts, let it be* for the edification of the church *that* you seek to excel." Put another way, Paul is saying to them, "You have been competing with one another to have the gifts; why not seek to excel in edifying the church by speaking in a known language?"

Tongues must be interpreted
Since prophecy is immediately understood by the hearers, it readily edifies them. Paul's preference is that his readers desire this gift to tongues. Tongues, however, is also a gift from God. Paul has not forbidden his readers from speaking in tongues, if indeed that is the gift of God to them. This he has made clear in verse 5. All he has been stressing is the need to think of edifying others by speaking in such a way that they can understand. He now needs to say something to those who claim to have the gift of tongues.

He says, in verse 13, "Therefore let him who speaks in a tongue pray that he may interpret." The tongue, being a language not understood by the hearers, will not be able to edify them. It therefore needs to be interpreted. It may be that some others present are able to understand that language and have the ability to interpret it for the other hearers. This is also a gift from God, as has been made clear in 1 Corinthians 12:10, which says, "...to another the working of miracles, to another prophecy, to another discerning of spirits, to another *different* kinds of tongues, to another the interpretation of tongues." What if there is no one present who is able to interpret? The one who speaks in the tongue must then pray for the gift of interpretation.

It may sound strange that the one who speaks in a tongue needs to pray for the gift of interpretation. We have established the truth earlier that the one who speaks in a tongue knows what he is saying. He is actually speaking out what God has revealed to him. Since he knows what he is saying, why doesn't he just speak the same thing in the language that everyone knows? We must understand that not a few people have difficulty in expressing what they know. They are "tongue- tied" when it comes to expressing themselves. Knowing is one thing, expressing what they know is another. We do have friends who are like that. Perhaps some of our readers also have this difficulty. This being the case, we would understand that the person who had the gift of tongues would need the help of God to speak in the language that he and everyone else knew.

The more likely explanation, however, is to be found in the very irony of the situation. Here is someone who utters truth in a foreign language. Why doesn't he utter the same truth in a language known to everyone present? "Pray for the gift of interpretation," says Paul! The apostle is here employing the device of "holy sarcasm" to jolt us. We are going to see more of this before the end of this chapter. For the moment, we only wish to note that Paul is engaging in remonstration with the Corinthian Christians. He is almost exasperated with their childish and selfish attitude. This comes across clearly in the verses following.

He says, in verse 14, "For if I pray in a tongue, my spirit prays, but my understanding is unfruitful." We have already seen that the spirit is the inner being of man. The spirit is capable of understanding and knowing. In the earlier verses, Paul has stressed the importance of ensuring that others understand what is being said so that they may be edified. When a person speaks in a tongue, only he himself understands. The hearers do not understand him. All his speaking will therefore be understood by himself, and of course, by God. A difficult person may still insist on speaking in tongues. He may say that he wishes only to pray to God. Paul is here saying that the person may indeed be praying sincerely, in his spirit, to God, but his understanding remains unprofitable to others. What he understands is not understood by others. So what profit will it be to others? Remember that the emphasis being made throughout this passage is the need to edify others. Earlier, in verse 4, Paul had said, "He who speaks in a tongue edifies himself, but he who prophesies edifies the church." Here, in verse 14, he is saying that a person who prays in a tongue is only benefiting himself and not others.

That is the way we should understand the word "unfruitful". The understanding of the one praying bears no fruit. It produces no spiritual benefit. It is useless. That is the way the same word is used elsewhere in the Bible. It says in Ephesians 5:11, "And have no fellowship with the unfruitful works of darkness, but rather expose *them*." It says in Titus 3:14, "And let our people also learn to maintain good works, to *meet* urgent needs, that they may not be unfruitful." It says in 2 Peter 1:8, "For if these things (namely, faith, knowledge, self-control, etc.) are yours and abound, *you will be* neither barren nor unfruitful in the knowledge of our Lord Jesus Christ." The point is made.

We move on to verse 15, which says, "What is *the conclusion* then? I will pray with the spirit, and I will also pray with the understanding. I will sing with the spirit, and I will also sing with the understanding." If we read this verse without taking note of the context, we might think that the spirit and the understanding are opposed to each other. We will then have difficulty understanding what this verse is saying. Keeping the context in view, however, and remembering that Paul has been advocating the fruitful use of the understanding, no such difficulty will arise. What Paul means is that one should pray and sing so as to be understood by others. Literally, the spirit can pray and sing, but the understanding cannot pray and sing. The spirit is the inner being of man. It is his soul, expressing itself through the body. The total person can pray and sing, but the isolated faculty of understanding, or the mind, cannot possibly pray and sing. Paul, however, does not intend us to take the phrase literally. He is basically saying to us that the understanding should be used fruitfully just as the spirit acts fruitfully. The understanding should edify others just as the spirit is edified. In life, we often use such metaphorical expressions. We would say the hunter is "going into the jungle", or the fisherman is "going to sea". What we mean is that the hunter is going into the jungle to hunt, and the fisherman is going to the sea to catch fish. To "pray and sing with the understanding" means to pray and sing in such a way that people benefit by understanding.

The next two verses confirm the correctness of our interpretation of this verse. It says, in verses 16 to 17, 'Otherwise, if you bless with the spirit, how will he who occupies the place of the uninformed say "Amen" at your giving of thanks, since he does not understand what you say? For you indeed give thanks well, but the other is not edified.' It was the custom of the churches in those days, and it ought to be our custom today, to say a hearty "Amen" each time a person finished praying. The early churches did not practice a corporate prayer in which everyone prayed aloud at the same time. This is done in many churches today, but it was never the practice of the early churches. This passage, together with 1 Corinthians 14:26-40, which we will study next, teach the need to pray one at a time in a public meeting. That way, the other people present will be able to say "Amen" at the end of the prayer. That is because they have understood the prayer and are in agreement with it. They are, therefore, able to say to God, "So be it," which is what "Amen" means. How are the other people to say "Amen" if the prayer has been in a language unknown to them? Are they to blindly say "Amen" despite not knowing what has been prayed for? That is certainly not the sense of Paul's words here.

Paul ends this section by saying, in verses 18 to 19, "I thank my God I speak with tongues more than you all; yet in the church I would rather speak five words with my understanding, that I may teach others also, than ten thousand words in a tongue." Paul is saying that he would rather seek to edify others by speaking in a language known to them, thereby conveying to them instruction, than utter words that cannot be understood by them. He has the gift of speaking in many tongues, which he seemed to have used whenever he preached the gospel in foreign lands. In the church, however, he would rather speak in a language understood by the people.

4.4   Prophecy Convicts Non-believers (14:20-25)

Having explained and emphasised the importance of the understanding, Paul is now ready to give another reason why prophecy is greater than tongues. He has already shown that prophecy is greater than tongues because it edifies the church while the gift of tongues only edifies the individual speaker. That was covered in verses 1 to 5. From verses 6 to 19, he explained that the understanding is so important for there to be edification. In the present section, namely verses 20 to 25, he shows that prophecy is greater than tongues because it convicts non-believers. Prophecy, then, has these two advantages over tongues: it is able to edify believers, and it is able to convict non-believers.

By this time, Paul has almost spent himself. He has explained, in Chapter 12, that the unity of the body of Christ needs to be preserved. He has explained the great importance of love, over against gifts, in Chapter 13. In the present chapter, he has gone to great length explaining the importance of edifying others through their understanding. He is now exhausted. He is saddened by the whole situation. We can almost hear Paul sighing as he writes verse 20, "Brethren, do not be children in understanding; however, in malice be babes, but in understanding be mature."

He is saying to his readers, "Stop being children. Be babies, if you like, in things that are evil. But as far as your understanding goes, be grown-ups!" Three grades of maturity are referred to here: the stage of infancy, the stage of childhood, and the stage of adulthood. Paul does not want his readers to be children in understanding, but to be adults. However, in things evil, they are to be babies. They are to be as ignorant as possible, to be as innocent as possible, with regard to things evil. But in understanding the things of God, the church, and the use of the gifts, they are to be mature.

He goes on to say, 'In the law it is written: "With men of other tongues and other lips I will speak to this people; And yet, for all that, they will not hear Me," says the Lord.' This is a quotation from Isaiah 28:11-12, in which God made known His intention to send foreign nations to judge the stiff-necked nation of Israel. God had spoken clearly and plainly to the nation, but the Israelites had continued refusing to listen. He therefore sent the Assyrians to attack the Israelites. Despite this, God's people had continued in their unbelief. He finally sent the Babylonians to punish them. Paul draws from these incidents in the history of Israel the truth that unknown languages are a sign of judgment to unbelievers. He says, in verse 22, "Therefore tongues are for a sign, not to those who believe but to unbelievers; but prophesying is not for unbelievers but for those who believe." Unknown languages are a curse, not a blessing, to those who refuse to believe. When Christians spoke in unknown languages, as on the day of Pentecost, it was to benefit those who could understand those languages. Those who were unbelieving found it all so confusing, and they could only mock.

This reminds us of the teaching of the Lord in Matthew 13:10-17. You would remember that there, the disciples asked the Lord why he spoke in parables to the people. The Lord's answer was that the mysteries of the kingdom of heaven were being revealed to those who believed, but hidden from those who were unbelieving. The parables were the means of conveying truths and blessing to the believing. The same parables were a stumbling block and a curse to the unbelievers. The apostle Paul says the same thing in 2 Corinthians 2:15-16. He says that the preaching of the gospel is "the aroma of death *leading* to death" to those who are perishing, at the same time, that it is the "aroma of life *leading* to life" to those who are being saved. The preaching of the gospel accomplishes these two effects at one and the same time. It saves believers, and it condemns the unbelievers. Here, in 1 Corinthians 14:22, Paul is saying that tongues are meant to convey the gospel to those who would believe, but they are a sign of God's judgment upon the unbelieving. In the church, which is the assembly of believers, the Corinthian Christians should be prophesying instead of speaking in tongues.

Note, by the way, that the comparison with the Assyrians and Babylonians shows that the tongues under discussion are actually human languages. The comparison would break down, otherwise. The same word for "tongues" is used of the languages of those nations as it is of the gift under discussion. Paul moves smoothly from verse 21 to verse 22 because he is referring to human languages throughout.

The apostle now wishes to conclude this section. This is indicated by the "therefore" of verse 23. The earlier "therefore" of verse 22 should rightly be translated as "so then". It was more to link that verse with the earlier one. We have now the closing verses, 23 to 25, "Therefore if the whole church comes together in one place, and all speak with tongues, and there come in *those who are* uninformed or unbelievers, will they not say that you are out of your mind? But if all prophesy, and an unbeliever or an uninformed person comes in, he is convinced by all, he is convicted by all. And thus the secrets of his heart are revealed; and so, falling down on *his* face, he will worship God and report that God is truly among you."

The situation in Corinth was very much like churches today. In any church, there will be found visitors who are either non-believers or ignorant believers. Remember that Corinth was a busy port visited by traders from all over the world. When the church gathered together, there would have been curious non-believers who came in to find out what was happening. There would also be believers from other parts of the world who joined in the meetings. If the Corinthian Christians began to speak in various unknown languages, wouldn't these visitors think that they were mad? This is exactly what happens today. We can collect together countless testimonies of friends who have been stumbled by observing so-called tongue-speaking in Charismatic churches. They had gone to those churches to worship God, or to find out more about the Christian faith. The babbling that they heard had caused them to be confused. Many had even been frightened by what they observed. They had wondered whether the Christians were in some way possessed by spirits, like those in pagan religions.

If, instead of speaking in unknown languages, the Corinthian Christians proclaimed the truths of the gospel in a known language, the unbeliever or the ignorant believer would be convinced and convicted by what was said. The same is true today. The gospel is not to be found everywhere or anywhere. You cannot buy the gospel from the supermarket. You do not hear the word of God on the radio or television, at least not in most countries in the world. If visitors come to the church, it must be to hear the word of God declared. If they understand what is said, the secrets of their hearts will be revealed. They will acknowledge the presence of God in the midst of His people. There will be those who are converted through hearing the word, and they will join the church and worship God.

The proclamation of the word of God is badly needed today. Why waste time on speaking in unknown tongues? Souls are perishing for want of the gospel. So many believers are stunted in their faith because of not being fed the word of God. Why should we be clamouring for the gift of tongues? Why are we not desiring the greater gifts of preaching and teaching God's word?

Prophecy is greater than tongues because it edifies the church. Prophecy is greater than tongues because it convicts and convinces non-believers. We must seek to be understood, by speaking in a language known to the hearers, and not by speaking in unknown tongues.

4.5 Conclusion

We must draw to a close. The Charismatics are wrong in so many ways about their view of the gifts:

i They are wrong in claiming that tongues are some unintelligible, incoherent sounds. When challenged, some of them would claim that these are tongues of angels or some unknown languages. But they have never been able to prove their claim. What they utter is nothing but babbling and gibberish.

ii They are wrong in emphasizing feelings at the expense of truth. They wrongly equate their feelings with the "praying with the spirit" of 1 Corinthians 14:15. Many of those who "speak in tongues" actually go into a trance, in which their mind is emptied. This is contrary to the teaching of Scripture on the importance of being self-controlled and sober-minded.

iii They are wrong in claiming that tongue-speaking may be engaged in for personal edification while other gifts are meant for the edification of the church. This claim is made by taking verses 2, 4 and 14 out of context.

In our study on 1 Corinthians 13, we have seen that there are no more prophecy and tongues today. The gifts have been withdrawn because their purpose has been fulfiled with the completion of God's revelation in the Scripture. What then is the relevance of 1 Corinthians 14 to us? It is still God's word for us today, and we may learn from it a number of lessons. Although the gifts are no more, the principles underlying those gifts are still relevant to us. We learn, firstly, of the need to always think of edifying others. We are not to think selfishly of our own good but to think of building up the church. Secondly, we learn that understanding the truth is important if people are to be edified. We must therefore desire the greater gifts of preaching and teaching the word of God. Non-believers need to hear the gospel in order to be saved. Believers need to hear the word of God in order to be built up in the faith. We need, therefore, to learn to be effective teachers of the word.

Five

ORDER IN PUBLIC WORSHIP (1 Corinthians 14:26-40)

We are coming to the end of our study on 1 Corinthians 12-14, which is on the spiritual gifts. The Corinthian Christians were facing some problems with regard to the use of the revelatory gifts, and especially with the gift of tongues. Paul's approach in dealing with the problems has been patiently to lay the foundational principles before proceeding to deal with the practical issues. The following foundational principles have been carefully laid – in Chapter 12, "The church is one body"; in Chapter 13, "Love is indispensable"; in Chapter 14:1-25, "Prophecy is greater than tongues". In this last portion, which is 1 Corinthians 14:26-40, he is ready to deal with the immediate problems. He gives the Corinthian Christians practical instructions on how the revelatory gifts of prophecy and tongues are to be used in public worship.

One key word for the Christian life is "edification". Christians should not be petty, inward-looking and selfish. They should always be thinking of how to build up the faith of others. The apostle Paul is always striking this note. In 1 Corinthians 6:12, he says, "All things are lawful for me, but all things are not helpful. All things are lawful for me, but I will not be brought under the power of any." In 1 Corinthians 10:23, he says, "All things are lawful for me, but not all things are helpful; all things are lawful for me, but not all things edify." The same note is struck in his letter to the Ephesians. In writing about the gifts of Christ to the church, he says, "And He Himself gave some to be apostles, some prophets, some evangelists, and some pastors and teachers, for the equipping of the saints for the work of ministry, for the edifying of the body of Christ... according to the effective working by which every part does its share, causes growth of the body for the edifying of itself in love" (Ephesians 4:11, 12, 16).

With regard to spiritual gifts, edification means remembering these four things: first, no schism should be caused to the church by anything sinful or selfist; second, love should be shown more and more; third, there should be intelligibility in whatever is uttered in the church; and fourth, there should be decency and order. The first three points arise from the studies we have done so far on 1 Corinthians 12 to 14. The last point arises from 1 Corinthians 14:26-40, which we are studying now.

5.1   Decency And Order (14:26-35)

Every gift is for edification
Paul develops this last point, namely that there should be decency and order in the church, by reminding his readers of the key word, "edification". He says, in verse 26, "How is it then, brethren? Whenever you come together, each of you has a psalm, has a teaching, has a tongue, has a revelation, has an interpretation. Let all things be done for edification." The question at the beginning of this verse is meant to connect what has been said earlier with what is going to be said later. By asking, "How is it then, brethren?", Paul is asking the Corinthian Christians, "What is the conclusion?" The answer is obvious, "Let all things be done for edification!" The question also carries an inquiry, "What is the condition with you?" That is why Paul mentions the list of things which they have been contributing at their meetings – a psalm, a teaching, a

tongue, a revelation, an interpretation. The irony of the situation becomes obvious. Paul is saying to them, "All of you have something to contribute, but it is not for edification!"

If you were present when the letter was read out, would you not feel the sting in Paul's words? Or would you be so "thick-skinned" and obtuse as not to get what he is saying? Words are meant to be understood. We should not miss the point made here. Note, by the way, that the gift of tongues is included in the list in this verse, showing that it is meant also for the edification of the church. The Charismatics are wrong in claiming that the gift of tongues is meant for personal edification!

Tongue-speaking must be orderly
Every gift is meant for the edification of the church. Paul moves on to apply this truth to the gift of tongues. It says in verses 27-28, "If anyone speaks in a tongue, *let there be* two or at the most three, *each* in turn, and let one interpret. But if there is no interpreter, let him keep silent in church, and let him speak to himself and to God." Three conditions are laid down for tongues. The first condition is that only a maximum of three persons may speak at any one meeting. In fact, it is preferable to have only two persons speaking but, *at the most,* there could be three. The second condition is that each of these two or three persons should speak in turn, and not together at the same time. The third condition is that there should be an interpreter present, to interpret the unknown language into the language known by everyone.

What if there is no interpreter present? Paul's answer is that the person who intends to speak in a tongue should keep silent. Paul adds the remark that he is to speak to himself and to God! Note very carefully that Paul does not say the individual is to practise his tongue-speaking at home. That is not the plain meaning of the sentence. The person is still in the church. He has been told to keep silent. He is not even to mutter quietly in the tongue. The phrase "to speak to himself and to God" means, therefore, to engage in thinking of the things he had wished to say aloud.

But why should he be directing the thoughts to himself and to God? If he had wished to *pray* in a tongue, as is referred to in 1 Corinthians 14:14-15, he should be directing the prayer to God, and not to himself. If he had wished to *speak* in a tongue, he should be directing the revelation he has received from God to other people, and not to himself or to God. What Paul says, however, is that he should speak "to himself and to God". Clearly, Paul does not intend his readers to take these words literally. He is employing what we have called "holy sarcasm". Not all sarcasm is sinful, just as not all anger is sinful. The Lord was angry at sin and hypocrisy. He was also, sarcastic without being spiteful. He said to Nicodemus, "Are you the teacher of Israel, and do not know these things?" (John 3:10). In reference to the hypocrites who blew their trumpets about their charitable deeds, the Lord said, "Assuredly, I say to you, they have their reward" (Matthew 6:2). Elijah mocked at the prophets of Baal and said, "Cry aloud, for he *is* a god; either he is meditating, or he is busy, or he is on a journey, *or* perhaps he is sleeping and must be awakened" (1 Kings 18:27). Here, Paul is employing "holy sarcasm" to bring home a point. He says, "...let him speak to himself and to God".

Charismatics today do not seem to feel embarrassed by this passage. They practise tongue-speaking without realising that their "tongues" are not the tongues spoken of in the Bible. We have noted repeatedly that the tongues of the Bible were human languages, and not the senseless jabber of the Charismatics. Furthermore, they engage in their so-called tongue-speaking without regard to the conditions laid down in this passage. Often, more than three persons would "speak in tongues". When they engage in corporate prayer, the whole church would "speak in tongues" at the same time. The conditions laid down in this passage for speaking in tongues are clear. Only two, or at most three, may speak. It is to be done one at a time. An interpreter has to be present, without which no one should speak.

Prophesying must be orderly
The conditions laid down for prophecy are similar to those for tongues. Paul says in verses 29-31, "Let two or three prophets speak, and let the others judge. But if *anything* is revealed to another who sits by, let the first keep silent. For you can all prophesy one by one, that all may learn and all may be encouraged." You would notice that two of the conditions are exactly the same as those for tongues. Firstly, only a maximum of three persons may speak. Secondly, they are to do so one by one. The third condition is different from that for tongues. It is required that other people in the church should judge what has been uttered.

Just as with the words "spirit" and "mysteries" in 1 Corinthians 14:2, there is a tendency in many people to form too quick an opinion on what it means "to judge". Our Charismatic friends would like us to understand it as "sifting out the true from the false". That is because they have already made up their mind that the gift of prophecy continues to today, and the "prophecy" they utter may consist of truths that are mixed with errors. They claim that such "prophesying" does not contradict the authority of Scripture, and their "prophecy" is of the secondary, or "non-canonical", type which does not compete with the truths of the Bible. With such assumptions already in their mind, they form the conclusion that "to judge" is to pick out things that are true while rejecting those that are not.

We cannot accept such an understanding of the word. The word Greek *diakrino* is made up of the preposition *dia* (meaning "through") and the verb *krinein* (meaning "to judge"). It has many shades of meaning – including to separate throughout, discriminate, discern, decide, judge, contend, hesitate, and doubt (Vine). The word is used in a number of other places. In 1 Corinthians 11:31 it is used in reference to self-examination, and in 1 Corinthians 6:5 it is used in reference to arbitration. In Acts 15:9, 1 Corinthians 4:7 and James 2:4 it is used in reference to discrimination. The basic *meaning* of the word is to exercise the critical (thinking, reasoning) faculty. What is its *usage* in this instance? Is it to sift out truth from error, as the Charismatics are claiming? Or is it to exercise the critical faculty in some other ways?

To arrive at the correct answer, we must first note that prophecy in the Bible is a reference to the intelligible communication of truths from God to man. It says in verse 30, "But if *anything* is **revealed** to another who sits by, let the first keep silent." (Emphasis added.) Clearly, the utterances of the prophets are the *revelation* of God. As such, it can never be mixed with error.

Two common arguments have been raised against this time-honoured understanding of prophecy. First, there are those who would claim that prophecy may consist of ecstatic utterances, as in the case of Saul in 1 Samuel 19:24. It says in 1 Samuel 19:24, "And he also stripped off his clothes and prophesied before Samuel in like manner, and lay down naked all that day and all that night. Therefore they say, 'Is Saul also among the prophets?'" Saul's exceptional case, however, can never be used to determine the meaning of prophecy. For one thing, we are not told that he uttered unintelligible words. He in fact prophesied "in like manner", that is as the prophets there did. For another, he was under God's judgement for attempting to kill David. He was therefore rendered helpless and made a fool of himself in public. A case of God's judgement cannot be used to determine the normal meaning of the word "prophecy" nor of the act of prophesying.

The second argument raised against the biblical understanding of prophecy is that while God's revelation is itself inerrant and infallible (that is contains no error and is not capable of proving false), it may become mixed with the errors of the persons who are prophesying. Put in another way, God's pure words may become mixed with human errors in the process of transmission! This is an attempt to "strain out a gnat and swallow a camel" (Matthew 23:24). It fails to take into consideration God's sovereignty in ensuring that His revelation will be given correctly. It distorts the biblical concept of the inspiration of Scripture (2 Timothy 3:16-17; 2 Peter 1:21). It is an attempt to dilute the biblical meaning of prophecy. It is a dangerous opinion that will ultimately undermine trust in the reliability and authority of the Bible.

No, true prophecy cannot possibly be mixed with error! That being so, the hearers in Paul's time would not be sifting out truth from error. They were, in any case, not in a position to do so. The Bible was not yet completely written. Only the Old Testament, and possibly the Gospels, were in circulation at that time. The people would not be able to assess what was prophesied in the light of the *complete* revelation of God. True, we are told in Acts 17:11 that the Bereans searched the Scriptures daily to find out whether the things they heard from Paul were true. They searched only the Old Testament. But what exactly did they search for? They searched for confirmation of what Paul was claiming about the person and work Christ. We are told, in Acts 17:2-3, "Then Paul, as his custom was, went in to them, and for three Sabbaths reasoned with them from the Scriptures, explaining and demonstrating that the Christ had to suffer and rise again from the dead, and *saying*, 'This Jesus whom I preach to you is the Christ.'" The Bereans were non-Christians who heard the gospel and searched the Old Testament to see if what they were hearing were indeed true. As a result, many of them believed. In 1 Corinthians 14:29, we have people who were *already believers*, and they were hearing *new revelation* from God. The two situations are different.

Prophecy was basically the *forthtelling* of the will of God. It could include the *foretelling* of future events. If the events did not occur as foretold, the person who prophesied would be treated as a false prophet. This is the teaching of Deuteronomy 18:20-22. The Lord Himself warned of those who would come to Him on the last day claiming to have prophesied and cast out demons in His name, but He is going to disown them (Matthew 7:21-23). The apostle Paul often warned the churches of false teachers from outside the church as well as from within, who would attempt to draw away the disciples (Acts 20:29-31).

The churches in the New Testament time, however, had accredited prophets in their midst (Ephesians 4:11; Acts 11:28; 13:1; 21:10). The word "prophet" is used in reference to one who occupies the office. We do not believe that these recognised prophets were listened to with distrust. It would have been strenuous upon the worshippers in church to have to constantly weigh up the utterances of these prophets. No! The official prophets, like Agabus, were trusted individuals who uttered inspired words from God. Only strangers and the common people were subjected to such tests because of claiming the gift of prophecy. The official prophets are referred to in 1 Corinthians 14:29. They are the ones who would normally prophesy in the church. The believers would be listening with the intention of obeying what God is saying through them. "To judge" would include this element of listening with the intention of obeying.

Paul, however, has been discussing the gift of prophecy, which may be possessed by those who are not official prophets. This is clear from 1 Corinthians 11:4-5, the passage about "head coverings", which says, "Every man praying or prophesying, having *his* head covered, dishonours his head. But every woman who prays or prophesies with *her* head uncovered dishonours her head, for that is one and the same as if her head were shaved." This is also clear from 1 Corinthians 14:1 where Paul had said, "Pursue love, and desire spiritual *gifts*, but especially that you may prophesy." Paul is not forbidding the people exercising the gift, just as he does not forbid them speaking in tongues (1 Corinthians 14:5). He says, therefore, in verse 31, "For you can all prophesy one by one, that all may learn and all may be encouraged."

What are the people in church to do when someone in their midst desires to prophesy? Remember that often there were strangers in the midst of the Corinthian church – "the uninformed and the unbelievers" mentioned in verses 23 and 24 of the same chapter. This certainly adds to the difficulty of the situation. What if one of these men claims to be a prophet and wishes to prophesy? The Corinthian Christians are to weigh carefully the prophecy with the view of obeying the will of God that is being revealed, or to reject the person as a false prophet if his prophecy turns out to be untrue. "To judge" would, therefore, include this element of testing the prophecy of the person to determine whether or not he is a true prophet. This, then, is what it means "to judge" – it is to listen carefully with the view of obeying the will of God, and to reject the false prophet if his prophecy turns out to be untrue.

These two purposes of "judging" are taught in the Bible, but not that of sifting out truth from error. In 1 Thessalonians 5:20-21, for example, we have these words, "Do not despise prophecies. Test all things; hold fast what is good." The prophecies are "tested" with the intention of obeying what is said. In 1 John 4:1, we have, "Beloved, do not believe every spirit, but test the spirits, whether they are of God; because many false prophets have gone out into the world." Here, the prophecies are "tested" with the view of rejecting the false prophets. We conclude from these arguments that "to judge" in 1 Corinthians 14:29 carries the same meaning as "to test" in these other passages. It means to weigh carefully with the intention of obeying what is heard, or to reject the person as a false prophet if his prophecy turns out to be untrue.

What about those who say, "How can I keep silent? I have a revelation from God which must be spoken out!" Verse 32 gives the answer to such people, "And the spirits of the prophets are subject to the prophets." Put another way, Paul is saying, "You may be under divine influence, but it does not destroy self-control." That person has to keep silent if the three conditions for prophesying cannot be fulfilled.[1]

---

[1] Some cessationists make short work of the passage by claiming that the "others" of verse 29 is a reference to the other prophets, and the "judging" is a reference to determining who is to speak, and in what order. This is possible but not probable because it would necessitate: (i) the assumption that there were many official prophets in the church; and (ii) the unenviable task of making such "judgment" in the midst of a meeting.

To arrive at the correct understanding of 1 Corinthians 14:29-32, it would be necessary to take into consideration the following facts: (i) the "prophets" are a reference to those who occupy the office of a prophet (1 Corinthians 12:29; Ephesians 4:11), whose "prophecy" consists of infallible revelation from God (1 Corinthians 13:2); and (ii) the problem being dealt with throughout is the abuse of the gift of prophecy by ordinary members of the church, and not by the leaders of the church, which the prophets

Women must behave orderly

Paul goes on to say, in verse 33, "For God is not *the author* of confusion but of peace, as in all the churches of the saints." Tongue-speaking, prophecy, or anything else that disturbs peace, and creates confusion, cannot be of God. Everything must be done in an orderly way. This is a rule that applies to all the churches. No special pleading is allowed.

This rule applies also to the role of women in the church. It says, in verse 34, "Let your women keep silent in the churches, for they are not permitted to speak; but *they are* to be submissive, as the law also says." The feminist movement of the world has infected the churches, and there is such a strong cry today for "the equality of the sexes" to be seen. To avoid being unpopular, many preachers try to explain away the passage by claiming that the teaching is "culturally conditioned" – that it applies only to the culture of Paul's time. Culture, however, is not even alluded to in the passage. We may not simply explain away teachings which we do not like. Instead, two reasons are given by the apostle for this teaching.

The first reason has been given already in verse 33 – God is not the author of confusion but of peace. God requires men and women to play different roles in the churches. There is no implication of inferiority or superiority. We are all sinners in God's sight. We are all saved by God's grace through faith in Jesus Christ. There is no more Jew or Greek, slave or free, and male or female, for we are all one in Christ. The same apostle teaches this in Galatians 3:28. The oneness, however, has to do with our standing before God, and our salvation. It does not wipe out the difference between the sexes, just as it does not wipe away ethnicity and status in society. It is only when men and women willingly take up their God-given roles in the churches that there will be peace and harmony.

This is not to say that women have no place in gospel work. The Bible shows that women were actively involved in direct

---

are (Acts 13:1). The passage shows that, ordinarily, the prophets are the ones who prophesied. The ordinary members who occasionally prophesy (cf. 14:5) have to adhere to the same rules spelled out by Paul here.

gospel work (e.g. Romans 16:1-3, 6; 1 Corinthians 9:5; etc.). Today, women may be involved in teaching children and other women. In some missions situation, they may be involved in teaching a mixed group of people. What needs to be kept in mind is the necessity of male leadership under normal circumstances. It is God's will that the man should be the head of the home (Ephesians 5:22ff.). It is God's will that only men are to be leaders of the churches (1 Timothy 3:1-7; Titus 1:6). It is God's will that women are to keep silent in the churches. Difficult people will want to twist this teaching and say that women are not permitted to utter a single word under all circumstances. However, that is not what the passage says. What it teaches is that they are not to be seen in a position of authority – such as prophesying or speaking in tongues. That is what it means by "they are to be submissive". Confirmation of this may be found in 1 Timothy 2:11-12, where the same apostle equates teaching with authority, "Let a woman learn in silence with all submission. And I do not permit a woman to teach or to have authority over a man, but to be in silence."

The second reason why women are to keep silent is that the law of God requires it. We know that this is the *second* reason because the word "also" indicates so – "as the law also says" (verse 34). Paul does not say which law in particular, but it is clear that the law of God as contained in the Old Testament is meant. Male leadership was such a well-known truth that Paul found no necessity to quote any proof-text. Moreover, he had handled the matter in another context before, in 1 Corinthians 11:2-16. This reason alone ought to end all controversy. If it is taught in God's law, we must not argue about it. It is our duty to accept it willingly and obey. That is not the case with fallen people, however. Knowing the truth is one thing, submitting to it is another. Oh, stubborn people that we are!

Paul found it necessary to add, in verse 35, "And if they want to learn something, let them ask their own husbands at home; for it is shameful for women to speak in church." Earlier, in verse 31, Paul had said, "For you can all prophesy one by one, that all may learn and all may be encouraged." This applies to women as well. They may learn, and be encouraged. However, it is out of place for women to be obtrusive – that is to be pushy, to be too loud, to want to be heard. If there is anything that they cannot understand, or if there are queries in their mind, they are to ask their husbands at home. The word "shameful" is a strong one. It carries the idea of being immodest or impure. Paul is saying that it is disgusting for women to speak in church. Such strong language makes sense only when we understand that he is not referring to mere talking to one another in church, but rather to the sort of assertiveness that is so unbecoming of the fairer sex.

The peculiar power and usefulness of women depend on their femininity. Not all women are the same. Some are louder in speech than others. Some are more cheerful and out-going than others. Such differences do not make any of them less feminine. It is only when their attitude and behaviour are such as to blur the distinction between the sexes that problems arise. The moment they begin to assert themselves like men, they cease to become objects of admiration and affection. There their power and usefulness cease! There they go against God's will!

What about unmarried women, and widows, who have no husbands to ask? Again, we must be careful not to display a difficult spirit. The word of God is plain here. Women, whether married or unmarried ones, must maintain their femininity and stop being obtrusive. They can be useful – very useful! – in God's work without being assertive. Women are as necessary to the life of the churches as the men. How many pastors will be able to testify to that! The saying is true – Behind every successful man is a woman! So also, behind every blessed church are the sisters who serve the Lord well. We must thank God for godly women in the churches!

We must come back to the main thrust of Paul's words. He is still discussing the spiritual gifts. The principle taught here is that women must not assert themselves by speaking in a public meeting. It follows that they are not to engage in prophesying or tongue-speaking in the church. The Corinthian church appears to be facing this difficulty. The women are clamouring to exercise their gifts. (The feminist movement is not a modern phenomenon!) Paul is saying to them that it ought not to be the case.

We see the same problem in today's churches. Wherever the Charismatic movement has gained a foothold, there the women feature prominently in the meetings.

5.2   Closing Admonition (14:36-40)

Listen to God's word
The apostle Paul has finished dealing with the practical aspects of the gifts. He now closes with admonition. He asks, in verse 36, "Or did the word of God come *originally* from you? Or *was it* you only that it reached?" Put another way, Paul is saying, "You are not the oldest (or mother-) church, neither are you the only church." Humility is needed to consider how others have understood the word of God. The Corinthian Christians had behaved as though God was speaking to them alone. There was no necessity for them to compare their teaching with the other churches. Theirs was the most vibrant church, the most blessed, in which God was present in the most apparent way. So they thought of themselves! They could act contrary to the teaching and practice of other churches. That was when they began to go astray! Individuals who are too proud and self-centred tend to go astray very quickly. So also with churches that are too proud and independent!

We know that truth is not measured by numerical strength. The false religions in the world have more members than many faithful churches. It may be that a faithful church will find itself contending alone for the truth, while other churches have succumbed to errors of various kinds. In such a situation, the truth lies with the one church and not with the many apostate churches. Certainly, Paul is not saying here that the other churches are right simply because they are more in number whereas the Corinthian church is alone in its practice of prophesying and tongue-speaking. No, Paul is pointing out rather the importance of referring to the word of God for all their practices. He is asking the Corinthian church not to do things contrary to the word of God. The word of God is known to other churches besides the Corinthian one. The problem with the Corinthian church is that the word of God is being set aside while practices not sanctioned by God are being carried out.

Today, Charismatic churches have grown in number, and many people are being attracted to them. As noted already, numbers alone are no measure of truth. The truth has to be determined from the Bible. We would ask the Charismatic churches the same questions that Paul asked the Corinthian churches – "Did the word of God come originally from you? Or was it you only that it reached?" Generations of Bible-believing Christians have studied the word of God and come to the conclusion that the revelatory and sign gifts have been withdrawn. The various Confessions Of Faith that issued forth from the Reformation affirm that Scripture alone is to be the sole authority in all matters of faith and practice. Of course, there have been isolated groups of people who claimed to have the gifts of tongues and prophecy after the time of the apostles. Paul's questions could be directed at such groups, just as they may be directed at the Charismatics today. The Charismatic churches are not at liberty to introduce their own teachings and practices!

Paul goes on to say, in verses 37 and 38, "If anyone thinks himself to be a prophet or spiritual, let him acknowledge that the things which I write to you are the commandments of the Lord. But if anyone is ignorant, let him be ignorant." Here is Paul's "holy sarcasm" again! Pride, and arrogance, have marked the Corinthian Christians. There have been those who claimed themselves to be prophets. There have been those who claimed themselves to be spiritual. These people would likely be resistant to Paul's teaching. Paul is reminding the Corinthian Christians that he writes as an apostle of Jesus Christ. His words are the commandments of the Lord. His words should not be questioned, but heeded. If there are those who remain adamant in refusing to heed Paul's teaching, let then continue in their ignorance!

I wonder what effect this last point has on you. We ought to realise that it is a terrible thing to be ignored by God. When God ignores a person, it means that that person is being left to wallow in his sins. It means that God's displeasure rests on him, and there is the certainty of judgement upon him. That is what it amounts to when Paul says, "But if anyone is ignorant, let him be ignorant." It reminds us of similar passages in the Bible. It says in Ezekiel 3:27, "But when I speak with you, I will open your mouth, and you shall say to them, 'Thus says the Lord God.' He who hears, let him hear; and he who refuses, let him refuse; for they *are* a rebellious house." It is as the Lord said of the hypocrites, in Matthew 6:2, "Assuredly, I say to you, they have their reward." Paul says, in Romans 1:24, "Therefore God also gave them up..." I shudder while writing this!

Decently and in order
Paul has come to the end of his discussion on the spiritual gifts. He says in verse 39, "Therefore, brethren, desire earnestly to prophesy, and do not forbid to speak with tongues." This is a repetition of his earlier statements. In Chapter 12, verse 31, he had said, "But earnestly desire the best gifts..." In Chapter 14, verse 1, he had said, "Pursue love, and desire spiritual *gifts*, but especially that you may prophesy." In verse 5 of the same chapter, he said, "I wish you all spoke with tongues, but even more that you prophesied;..." At the time of writing, the gifts of prophecy and tongues were still available. Paul found it necessary to remind his readers that he was not trying to stifle their gifts. That was for the simple reason that, throughout, he had not been too enthusiastic about their abuse of the gifts. They had been elevating the gifts above the graces of faith, hope and love. They had been proud of their abilities. There was such chaos in the church as they exercised those gifts. Paul had been "putting on the brakes" instead of "stepping on the accelerator". He wanted them to be more sober and mature in their understanding and use of the gifts. They could prophesy and speak with tongues if the conditions spelled out earlier

were fulfilled.

A closing point is now given, in verse 40, "Let all things be done decently and in order." The word "decently" means appropriately, in a manner that is pleasing to all who are of right mind. To do things "in order" means to do them in the proper place, at the proper time, in the proper way. This is a general principle that is applicable to all Christians, and in all situations in the church. It is mentioned as a last point to finish this section on the use of the gifts. It is the last knot that clinches the point that *there should be order in public worship*.

5.3   Conclusion

The gifts of prophecy and tongues have ceased, but the principles underlying their practice remain. The truth we should grasp from this study is that there can be no edification unless there is orderliness. All church meetings must therefore be planned carefully in advance, and all the items should be thought through before being presented. We are not advocating a rigid inflexibility under all circumstances. We are not denying that God can prompt a person to say things quite unplanned for. All that we are pointing out is the need to do everything in a decent and orderly way.

This rule of "decency and orderliness" is always broken by the Charismatics in their meetings. In the first place, they have been wrong in their understanding of what constitute tongues and prophecy. Their "tongues" are not human languages, and their "prophecies" are made up of truths mixed with errors. When practising their "tongue-speaking" and "prophesying", the conditions laid down in Scripture are never followed. More than three people speak, often at one and the same time. Women occupy a prominent place in their meetings.

God's word is clear. It is sufficient for all our needs. It shows up very clearly the errors of the Charismatic movement. We should learn to trust the word of God more and more. If we love the Lord, we would love His word. We should exert effort to study His word, and prayerfully seek to understand it correctly. We must also preach the word of God, and never be diverted by charismania!

Six

TONGUES, HEALINGS AND MIRACLES
(Mark 16:9-20)

Our studies on 1 Corinthians 12-14 have shown that the revelatory gifts of tongues, prophecy and special knowledge have ceased. We now have the completed Scripture to guide us in all matters of faith and practice. This view, derived from the Bible itself, has been called *Cessationism*. The Cessationist position has been attacked by opponents in various ways. The approach is often to caricature the Cessationist position instead of by providing a more convincing exposition of Scripture.

One such attack takes the form of labelling all Cessationists as Dispensationalists. While most Dispensationalists would hold to the Cessationist position, it is not true that all Cessationists are Dispensationalists. Dispensationalism holds to the view that God's programme for the world consists of several distinct periods, or "dispensations". According to the majority-view of Dispensationalism, there are seven such periods in which people are saved in different ways – by believing in the promises of God, by keeping the laws of Moses, and so on. To them, the Old Testament saints were not regenerated by the

Holy Spirit. The nation of Israel constituted the people of God, distinct from the New Testament church. A premillennial return of Christ is held in which there is "the great tribulation" sandwiched between "the rapture" and "the revelation". These views are not subscribed to by very many Cessationists.

Our concern here is with other forms of attack that appear valid because the Scripture is appealed to. Our opponents claim that their beliefs on tongues, prophecy and healings are based on certain passages of Scripture, which we will need to examine. They also claim that the Cessationists limit the power of God, allowing for no possibility of God performing miracles today. They also accuse the Cessationists of being "cerebral", that is being cold and academic, and giving no place to the feelings. We will answer these accusations by appealing to the Scripture itself.

6.1   Signs Of The Apostles

Mark 16:17-18
One passage often appealed to by the Charismatics for their tongue-speaking and healing practices is Mark 16:17-18. The passage says, "And these signs will follow those who believe: In My name they will cast out demons; they will speak new tongues; they will take up serpents; and if they drink anything deadly, it will by no means hurt them; they will lay hands on the sick, and they will recover." The claim is that believers are promised by the Lord the ability to perform these signs, the purpose of which is to convince non-believers of the truth of the gospel.

We have learned of the three basic rules of interpreting the Bible – first, to take the words of Scripture plainly; second, to take the words in context; and third, to compare scripture with scripture. Applying the first rule, that of "plain sense", the passage shows that, (i) believers – all believers, without exception – should be able to do the things promised; and (ii) all the signs – not just one or two of them – should be capable of being performed by the believer. No exception is indicated in the passage.

The plain meaning
These, however, are not true of the Charismatics. Not all of them are able to speak in tongues, despite being taught how to have the "gift". This has cause many of them to be confused and to wonder why it is that the gift is denied them. Can it be that they are not true believers? Can it be that they are loved less by God compared to others? Can it be that they lack faith? Can it be that they have not desired the gift strongly enough? Or is it because they have not used the right method to obtain the gift? What is the right method anyway? Where in the Scripture do we find the *method* of getting the gift taught?

Furthermore, those who claim to have the gift of tongues do not have all the other gifts mentioned in Mark 16:17-18. They may say, "But I am satisfied to have just the gift of tongues. I know of others who have the gifts of healings and casting out demons." We would question, however, such claims. In the first place, we question whether their so-called "tongues" are human languages. It is easy to say that they know of others who speak in certain languages, but were they present when those languages were spoken? And if they were present, can they be sure that what they heard were truly the languages claimed to be? Many Charismatics have attended healing rallies in which various claims have been made. Again, we would question whether true healings and true exorcism had been performed. What we hear of are things that cannot be verified – the curing of head and stomach aches, the lame being made able to limp (not to walk!), the partially blind being made able to see better, and the partially deaf being made to hear better. Testimonies abound of those who have been healed of cancer and leukemia, but what has not been told is that those same persons die of those same diseases not long after.

Why do the Charismatics claim the gift of tongues, and even of healing and the casting out of demons, and not the other gifts mentioned in Mark 16:17-18? When they are bitten by poisonous snakes, would they claim the promise of this passage and not rush to hospital to get an injection? When they accidentally drink poison, would they stay home calmly and expect to live? The ridiculous claims of the Charismatics are obviously not consistent with the plain meaning of this passage of Scripture.

The correct context
The Charismatics have also failed to apply the other rules of interpretation to the passage – namely, those of "correct context" and "the analogy of Scripture". The rule of "correct context" would require us to understand the passage in the light of the occasion and circumstances in which those words of the Lord were uttered. We would need, therefore, to look at the verses before and after the passage in question. The proper context would require that we consider the passage from verse 9 to the end of the chapter. Some scholars have questioned whether this passage should be regarded as part of Scripture, claiming that it was added later and did not form part of the original Gospel of Mark. Until convincing evidence is given to prove that, we should regard Mark 16:9-20 as part of Scripture.

The context shows that the disciples of the Lord, namely the eleven apostles, had great difficulty believing that the Lord was risen. We are told in verses 9 to 11, "Now when *He* rose early on the first day of the week, He appeared first to Mary Magdalene, out of whom He had cast seven demons. She went and told those who had been with Him, as they mourned and wept. And when they heard that He was alive and had been seen by her, ***they did not believe***." (Emphasis added.)

We are told in the next two verses, "After that, He appeared in another form to two of them as they walked and went into the country. And they went and told it to the rest, but ***they did not believe them either***." (Emphasis added.)

We are told, immediately after that, "Later He appeared to the eleven as they sat at the table; ***and He rebuked their unbelief*** and hardness of heart, ***because they did not believe*** those who had seen Him after He had risen." (Emphasis added.)

Three times we are told that the disciples did not believe

the Lord was risen. We are told also that the Lord was not pleased with their unbelief. It was in this situation that the Lord appeared before them to give them the Great Commission. It says, in verses 15 and 16, "And He said to them, 'Go into all the world and preach the gospel to every creature. He who believes and is baptised will be saved; but he who does not believe will be condemned.'" The phrases, "he who believes" and "he who does not believe", refer to the hearers of the gospel.

The Lord then addressed the apostles, who were receiving this Great Commission, saying, in verses 17 and 18, "And these signs will follow those who believe. In My name they will cast out demons; they will speak with new tongues; they will take up serpents; and if they drink anything deadly, it will by no means hurt them; they will lay hands on the sick, and they will recover." The Lord had just rebuked the disciples for not believing that He was risen from the dead. As these words were uttered, we can almost see Him lifting His gaze away from them into the distance sadly. The phrase, "those who believe", here means those of the apostles who believe that He was risen. Of course, the Lord expected every one of the apostles to believe Him, but He had first to rebuke their unbelief and then give them the promise of the accompanying signs when they obeyed Him.

The people referred to in verse 16, therefore, are different from those referred to in verses 17 and 18. The former are hearers of the gospel, the latter are the apostles who are being commissioned to proclaim that gospel. It follows that the signs mentioned are meant only for the apostles, and not for all who believe in the gospel. Confirmation of this is found in the subsequent verses. We read in verses 19 and 20, "So then, after the Lord had spoken to them, He was received up into heaven, and sat down at the right hand of God. *And they went out and preached everywhere, the Lord working with them and confirming the word through the accompanying signs.* Amen." (Emphasis added.)

Comparing with other scriptures
We have still to apply the third rule of interpretation, that of "the analogy of Scripture". The Great Commission is given in a fuller form in Matthew 28:18-20. The Lord says, "All authority has been given to Me in heaven and on earth, go therefore and make disciples of all the nations, baptizing them in the name of the Father and of the Son and of the Holy Spirit, teaching them to observe all things that I have commanded you; and lo, I am with you always, *even* to the end of the age." This parallels the version recorded in Mark 16:15-16, which was given on a different occasion. We find that, in Matthew 28, there is absolutely no mention of the sign-gifts to those who believe the gospel. This shows that Mark 16:15-16 alone constitute the Great Commission, while verses 17 and 18 were applicable only to the apostles who were receiving that commission.

Further confirmation may be found in other parts of the New Testament. The Great Commission was given on another occasion in a different form in Acts 1:8, which says, "But you shall receive power when the Holy Spirit has come upon you; and you shall be witnesses to Me in Jerusalem, and in all Judea and Samaria, and to the end of the earth." This verse tells us that the apostles would become witnesses to the Lord. The word "witnesses" is not to be understood in the loose sense that we use it today of those who preach the gospel. Here, "witnesses" carry the idea of those who were officially appointed to testify to known facts, such as the ones we find in the law courts today. The apostles were appointed by Christ to testify to the fact that He was risen, and to declare that He was indeed the Saviour who was prophesied of in the Old Testament. We are told, in Acts 1:2-3, "He through the Holy Spirit had given commandments to the apostles whom He had chosen, to whom He also presented Himself alive after His suffering by many infallible proofs, being seen by them during forty days and speaking of the things pertaining to the kingdom of God."

Similarly, when another apostle was to be appointed to re-place Judas, the qualifications needed were spelled out as follows, "Therefore, of these men who have accompanied us all the time that the Lord Jesus went in and out among us, beginning from the baptism of John to that day when He was taken up from us, one of these must become a witness with us of His resurrection" (Acts 1:21-22). Another example should suffice. When Peter preached on the day of Pentecost, he said, "This Jesus God has raised up, of which we are all witnesses."

Authenticating the apostles
We see, then, that the apostles were the specially chosen instruments of Christ to bear witness to Him. To them were given the special signs mentioned in Mark 16:17-18. When Paul was appointed to be an additional apostle, specially assigned to proclaim the gospel to the Gentiles, he was given a vision of the risen Christ while on the road to Damascus (Acts 9). He referred to that experience in later years, claiming that he was a true apostle (1 Corinthians 15:8-9; Galatians 1:1, 15-16). When challenged about the authenticity of his apostleship, he said, in 2 Corinthians 12:12, "Truly the signs of an apostle were accomplished among you with all perseverance, in signs and wonders and mighty deeds." Paul was appealing to the miraculous deeds which he performed among the Corinthian Christians in an earlier visit as proof of his apostleship.

If the miraculous deeds of Mark 16:17-18 were signs of the apostles, how can they be performed by non-apostles today? Those who claim the ability to speak in tongues, to heal, and to cast out demons will have to claim also that they are apostles. We know, however, that the apostles and prophets (the Old Testament ones included) were appointed by God to reveal His will. We are told, in Ephesians 2:19-20, "Now, therefore, you are no longer strangers and foreigners, but fellow citizens with the saints and members of the household of God, having been built on the foundation of the apostles and prophets, Jesus Christ Himself being the chief corner*stone*..." The teaching of the apostles and prophets constitutes the foundation of faith. Their teaching arises from Christ, and depends on Him, who is the chief cornerstone of that foundation. The apostles were given the ability to perform miracles so as to convince all that they were true messengers of Christ.

Authenticating the apostolic message
The apostles were helped in their ministry by other men. Some of them were prophets, others were evangelists, and some were deacons (Acts 6:8; 8:5-6; 11:28; 13:1; 21:10). Whatever their official positions may have been in the church, a limited number of such men were also given the ability to perform signs and wonders, the purpose of which was to confirm the message proclaimed by the apostle – that Jesus Christ is the promised Saviour of the world. This was "the mystery kept secret since the world began", which was now being revealed (Romans 16:25-26; Ephesians 3:2-6; Colossians 1:25-27). This purpose of the sign-gifts is declared in Hebrews 2:3-4, "...how shall we escape if we neglect so great a salvation, which at the first began to be spoken by the Lord, and was confirmed to us by those who heard *Him*, God also bearing witness both with signs and wonders, with various miracles, and gifts of the Holy Spirit, according to His own will?"

We see, then, that the miraculous signs served two basic purposes: (i) to show that the apostles were special witnesses of Christ; and (ii) to show that the message they and their colleagues were proclaiming was authentic. These two purposes have been fulfilled. There are no more apostles around today. The foundation of the church, namely the written word of God, has been laid. How can there be people around today who have the miraculous gifts?

We do well to remember the words of the Lord in Matthew 7:21-23, "Not everyone who says to Me 'Lord, Lord,' shall enter the kingdom of heaven, but he who does the will of My Father in heaven. Many will say to Me in that day, 'Lord, Lord, have we no prophesied in Your name, cast out demons in You name, and done many wonders in Your name?' And then I will declare to them, 'I never knew you; depart from Me, you who practise lawlessness!'"

6.2   God Is Able!

The accusation is often made against Cessationists that they limit the power of God. The claim is that since God is all-powerful and unchanging, He is able to perform signs, wonders and miracles today, just as He was able to do so in the past.

Here, the Charismatics have confused the ability of God with the purposes of God. God has not changed. He continues to be God, who is all-knowing, all powerful, and unchanging in His divine essence. He is in sovereign control of all creation, and He is able to suspend "the laws of nature" so that a miracle occurs. We are not questioning the ability of God at all. We are not limiting His power. We are only questioning the Charismatic understanding of the purposes of God.

The ability and purposes of God
God does not act the same way in all circumstances, and in all ages. He commanded Moses to climb up Mount Sinai to get the two tables of the Law. He did not require the other prophets to do the same. He certainly does not require us to do the same today. God allowed His Son, Jesus Christ, to die on the cross of Calvary as a sacrifice for the sins of His people. He does not require that believers today do the same. Those were events unique to the persons and the times concerned. There is a sense in which we are to imitate the Lord, but not in *this* sense. Although these events are recorded in Scripture, they are not meant to be followed in a crass and literal manner. This is where the correct rules of interpreting Scripture need to be followed. The Bible is not a book of magic and charms. It is a book that reveals God and His will to us. It is meant to be used intelligently.

The Old Testament scriptures paved the way for the New. The Old Testament prophets foretold the coming of the Saviour. The Old Testament sacrifices foreshadowed the atoning death of Christ. When Jesus Christ came into the world, He fulfilled all the prophecies of the Old Testament concerning His person and work. He ushered in a new age in which the gospel is to be proclaimed to all nations (that is, all ethnic groups), in which all who are to be saved will be called out of the world into His kingdom. This "age of grace", or "age of the gospel", began with the first coming of Christ and will end with the second coming of Christ. More precisely, this period began with the pouring out of the Holy Spirit upon the disciples on the day of Pentecost, and it will end with the day of judgement. The Bible calls this period "the last days".

The uniqueness of "the last days" is made clear by the apostle Peter in Acts 2:16-21. He applied Joel's prophecy to the period which began on the day of Pentecost, saying in verses 16-18, "But this is what was spoken by the prophet Joel: 'And it shall come to pass in the last days, says God, that I will pour out of My Spirit on all flesh; your sons and your daughters shall prophesy, your young men shall see visions, your old men shall dream dreams, and on My menservants and on My maidservants I will pour out My Spirit in those days; and they shall prophesy.'" These are words of prophecy, couched in Old Testament imagery. It will not be right for us to press for a literal, word-for-word correspondence with the events of Pentecost. The main thrust of the prophecy is that the beginning of the gospel age would be marked by signs, wonders and miracles. Peter understood it that way.

We are told further, in Acts 2:19-20, that "the last days" will end with signs. The signs, however, will not be seen in God's people as was the case at the beginning but in the heavenly realms and on earth. The passage says, "I will show wonders in heaven above and signs in the earth beneath; blood and fire and vapour of smoke. The sun shall be turned into darkness, and the moon into blood, before the coming of the great and awesome day of the LORD." This is exactly the language used by the Lord when He spoke of His second coming in Matthew 24:29-31. This is also the language employed by the apostle John in Revelation 6:12-17, when he described what will happen on judgment day.

Joel's prophecy, quoted by Peter in Acts 2, ends with the words, "And it shall come to pass that whoever calls on the name of the LORD shall be saved." This corresponds with the "Great Commission" of Matthew 28:18-20, in which the gospel is to be preached to all peoples in the world. People from all nations will be saved. Non-Jews as well as Jews will become the people of God. Local churches, made up of believers from all ethnic backgrounds, will be established. The traditional barrier between Jews and Gentiles will be broken down (Galatians 3:14, 26-29; Ephesians 2:14-18). We see, then, that the gospel age began with signs and it will end with signs. It is a unique age which stands in great contrast to the Old Testament age.

:14-18 *The signs of tongues and prophecy*
During the Old Testament time, the nation of Israel constituted the people of God. God made His covenant with that nation, raised up prophets from the nation, gave His law to the nation, and promised that the Saviour would arise from the nation (Romans 9:4-5). Those who were not Israelites by birth had to be absorbed into the nation of Israel in order to become God's people. Non-Jews, like Ruth, had to adopt the Jewish way of life and to worship the God of the Israelites. Up to the time of Christ, there were Gentiles who attached themselves to the temple and synagogues. These were known as "proselytes" (Acts 2:10; 13:43).

With this background in mind, we understand why it was so difficult for the Jews to accept the fact that the old order was being swept away with the dawning of the new age. The apostles themselves needed to be persuaded of this change. They had been told by the Lord, "You shall receive power when the Holy Spirit has come upon you; and you shall be witnesses to Me in Jerusalem, and in all Judea and Samaria, and to the end of the earth" (Acts 1:8). This was, of course, a reference to the day of Pentecost, when the Holy Spirit was poured out on the gathered disciples. The power of the Holy Spirit was to enable the disciples to proclaim the gospel to all nations – beginning in Jerusalem, to all Judea and Samaria, and to the end of the earth. This was the "greater works" mentioned by

111

the Lord in John 14:12, which the disciples would do. The works would be greater in extent and scope – covering more than the land of Israel, and involving more than just the Jews.

When the promise of Acts 1:8 began to be fulfilled, the Jewish disciples continued to have difficulty believing that other nations would be incorporated into the church, on an equal footing with them. Jews and proselytes the disciples could accept; the Samaritans the disciples could possibly accept; but not outright Gentiles! Although the Samaritans were a despised half-caste, who had Jewish blood in them, they worshipped the same God as the Israelites did, and believed in the coming of the Saviour (John 4:1-26). To the Jews, the Gentiles were worse than the Samaritans. This accounts for why the gift of tongues was given to the Samaritan believers in Acts 8:14-17 and to the Gentile believers in Acts 10:44-48. It was to convince the Jews that there could be true believers from other nations, who would be treated as equal to the Jewish believers.

We are told in Acts 10:44-45, "While Peter was still speaking these words, the Holy Spirit fell upon all those who heard the word. And those of the circumcision who believed were astonished, as many as came with Peter, because the gift of the Holy Spirit had been poured out on the Gentiles also." On this basis, Peter said, "Can anyone forbid water, that these should not be baptised who have received the Holy Spirit just as we *have*?" Later, at the church council in Jerusalem, Peter affirmed the same thing, saying, "Men and brethren, you know that a good while ago God chose among us, that by my mouth the Gentiles should hear the word of the gospel and believe. So God, who knows the heart, acknowledged them by giving them the Holy Spirit, just as *He did* to us, and made no distinction between us and them, purifying their hearts by faith" (Acts 15:7-9).

The gift of tongues to the hearers *en masse*, that is, all together at the same time, was a sign that a new age had arrived. A similar experience was encountered by the apostle Paul when he met with a group of "disciples" in Ephesus (Acts

19:1-7). These men were either disciples of John the Baptist who departed from Israel before the Messiah was revealed to the public (John 1:29-36; 3:22-36), or disciples of a disciple of John the Baptist. They had known only "John's baptism". They were looking forward to the coming of the Messiah, not knowing that He had already come. They were, as it were, Old Testament believers living in the New Testament age. When Paul proclaimed to them about the Christ who had come, they were baptised "in the name of the Lord Jesus", meaning that they had become Christians. When Paul laid hands on them, they received the Holy Spirit. This was indicated by their tongue-speaking and prophesying. On this occasion, the signs were given more for the benefit of the believers than of Paul, for Paul had already understood that the gospel was to go to all nations (Acts 9:15-16; Colossians 1:26-27). The Ephesian disciples needed to be convinced that a new age had dawned.

These are the only instances recorded in Scripture in which the hearers spoke in tongues and prophesied *en masse*. They were the "first fruits" of the gospel age. The mass tongue-speaking and prophesying were signs of the beginning of the gospel age, given to convince the doubting Jewish Christians. Once the purpose was fulfilled, the signs were not repeated. The three thousand souls who believed through the preaching of Peter on the day of Pentecost did not show the signs (Acts 2:40-47). The multitudes of people converted through Paul's ministry on other occasions did not show these signs. The *gifts* of tongue-speaking and prophesying were possessed by some individuals, as was the case in the Corinthian church, to reveal God's will. These gifts were *revelatory* in nature. When given *en masse*, as happened in the few instances recorded in the book of Acts, they constituted signs of the beginning of "the last days".

The signs are not meant to continue all through the gospel age. Neither are they meant to teach believers today the need of a baptism of the Spirit after conversion. Revivals may occur, as have occurred on many occasions in different parts of the world, in which many are converted at the same time. In such times of intensified activity of the Holy Spirit, the works of grace in the souls of convicted sinners may appear dramatic – for example, weeping over sins, writhing in agony of soul, shouting for joy over sins forgiven, and so on. Wise counsellors will not encourage nor give too much credence to such outward manifestations, but will look instead for the inward and lasting changes wrought by the Holy Spirit. Yes, mass conversions can take place, as happened on the day of Pentecost, but the signs of tongue-speaking and prophecy are not expected to be seen. The teaching of Scripture is that the baptism, or reception, of the Spirit occurs at conversion, without being accompanied by tongue-speaking and prophesying (Galatians 3:2; also Romans 8:9, 11; 1 Corinthians 12:13).

The ability of God is one thing; the purpose of God is another.

6.3   Subjective Experiences

Since God is able to perform miracles, will He ever perform any today? There are "Cessationists" of sorts today who would dogmatically give a negative answer to that question. Theirs, however, is not the view of classical Cessationism. The traditional Reformed view is that God may work miracles according to His sovereign will, although He does not do so through men who are gifted with that ability. In this regard, it is important to be clear concerning the different issues that are involved.

God's sovereignty and the authority of Scripture
One area of distinction to be made is the difference between the authority of God over all creation and the authority of His word to believers. Put another way, there is a difference between the sovereignty of God over His creation and the submission of His creatures to His authority. God rules over the whole creation, and the so-called laws of nature are His way of keeping the universe going. He is able to suspend these laws at His will so that things do not work the way they normally do. When this happens in the life of an individual, a miracle

is said to have occurred. Since God is unchanging, He continues to be able to perform miracles. There is no indication in Scripture that He has chosen to suspend the performance of miracles of every kind. Our understanding of the sovereignty of God will have to allow for the possibility of God performing miracles when, where and how He wishes.

God has chosen to reveal Himself and His will in the Scripture. His sovereignty extends over the writing of scriptures and the preservation of those scriptures. The completed revelation testifies to its own divine origin, authenticity and sufficiency. God is faithful and His word cannot be broken. He cannot act contrary to what He has declared in Scripture. All true Evangelicals hold to the sole authority of Scripture in all matters of doctrine and practice. What Scripture says is what God desires of His people to believe and do. We have seen that signs, wonders and miracles serve certain purposes that were already accomplished at the beginning of the New Testament age. The revelatory gifts were given to some individuals at that time and have been withdrawn. No man may claim to have the revelatory or sign gifts – to perform them when, where and how he pleases. To do so would be to act contrary to the teaching of Scripture. It will be to call into question the sufficiency of Scripture. It will be to undermine the sole authority of Scripture in the life of the believer.

The Cessationist position is based on the principle of the sole authority of Scripture. It does not necessarily rule out the ability, and possibility, of God performing miracles in this age.

Guidance sought, guidance given
A related matter is the difference between *guidance sought* and *guidance given*. A believer may seek guidance from God through prayer, consultation with other men, the application of Scripture to the situation, and the consideration of God's providential dealings in the circumstance. He may ask God to give clear guidance in decision-making, but he may not determine the will of God by pre-determined signs. The casting of lots, and the like, to determine God's will belong to the pre-

Pentecost age (e.g. Acts 2:26; Judges 6:36-40). In a crisis, he may ask God to intervene miraculously, but he should not dictate to God how He should act. God is in sovereign control over nature and the life of the believer, and He has given the completed Scripture which is sufficient to guide us in all our needs. That is so far as the seeking of guidance from God is concerned.

The giving of guidance by God to a believer is another matter. God may act miraculously in extraordinary circumstances for the good of His people, and to the glory of His name. These extraordinary actions might include the giving of a vision, a healing – yes, even a tongue or a prophecy. Or, more likely, it may be an extraordinary intervention of some kind to deliver His people from a crisis that involves life or faith. When this happens, the believer should not be surprised nor alarmed. After all. we believe in a living God who is in sovereign control over all creation. We trust in a heavenly Father who cares for His children. A miraculous divine intervention should cause the believer to be thankful to God, and to resolve to lead a more consecrated life. It should humble the community of God's people and lead to a sense of awe and praise. It is not meant to be paraded triumphalistically in public as "a testimony", or bandied around in dramatic and pietistic tones.

God does intervene miraculously in the lives of His people, although His people should not be surviving on a diet of signs, wonders and miracles.

The place of feelings
Another area of differentiation is the role which feelings play compared with the teachings of Scripture in the life of the believer. God made man a being that is rational, emotional and volitional. Put another way, he is capable of understanding, feeling and acting. He has the faculties of mind, heart and will. All three faculties are important. The teaching of Scripture is that the mind must have the priority (Romans 12:2; 2 Timothy 1:7). The feelings must not be suppressed, lest we become cold and judgmental. Neither should they be allowed

to dominate, lest we become frothy and emotional. Instead, the feelings must be regulated, or controlled, by the truth of Scripture. It follows that the mind should be filled with truth so as to guide and regulate the feelings. Effort should be made to study, to think over, and to understand the word of God. Doctrine should not be despised.

What about "impressions"? An impression is a sudden thought that comes to a person in a compelling manner. It, therefore, involves the mind and the heart. Are impressions to be trusted? Just as God may give a vision or perform a miracle, He can guide by an impression (Acts 16:6-10). Man has a subjective as well as a rational faculty. He has a soul, which is spirit in essence. The Holy Spirit dwells in the believer and interacts directly with the soul (1 Corinthians 2:11-16). God's normal way of acting is to guide the believer via the mind, that is by the understanding of truth. By His Spirit, He may cause a thought to bear strongly upon the soul. The believer should obey that impression, *if it is in accord with the teachings of Scripture*. The impression may be to do good to a stranger, to witness to a colleague, to pray for a distant friend, or something else of like nature.

The qualification, "if it is in accord with the teachings of Scripture", should be noted. The Holy Spirit may prompt us to act in a certain way in any particular moment of our life, but He will not prompt us to act contrary to the teachings of Scripture. The *source* of authority is the Scripture. The *agency*, or *instrumentality*, of that authority is the Holy Spirit illuminating the mind with regard to truth and giving the believer the desire to obey the truth. The illumination may come to the believer as an impression, or it may come to the believer when he seeks to know and obey the truth. In the one case, the Holy Spirit takes the initiative in giving the impression. In the other case, the believer takes the initiative to understand truth and is given illumination by the Spirit.

The devil may impersonate the Holy Spirit as the agent of an impression. He is capable of transforming into an angel of light (2 Corinthians 11:3, 14-15). He primarily attacks the mind, shooting at it with fiery darts (Ephesians 6:16). Since he is a deceiver, he will attempt to sow doubts, errors and evil thoughts in the mind of the believer. He will attempt to cloud the believer's perception of the truth and shake his faith, as happened to Eve in the garden of Eden. He will misapply truth and prompt the believer to act according to his wiles, as happened to the Lord in the wilderness (Matthew 4). Knowing the truth will prevent us from succumbing to perversions of the truth. It will help us to distinguish between the genuine impressions given by the Holy Spirit and the goading of the devil, who is opposed to the truth.

A believer who keeps a close walk with his Lord will have many precious experiences of divine interventions and guidance. He will not be one who seeks such experiences for their own sake. Instead, he will be one who sees the importance of knowing the word of God and obeying it. Increasingly, he will learn the difference between the mistaken impulses of his sinful self and the spiritual guidance of the Spirit, based on the objective word of God. The filling, and leading, of the Spirit is experienced more by the knowledgeable and obedient than by the ignorant and disobedient (John 14:23; 1 John 1:3-4).

6.4   Conclusions On The Spiritual Gifts

The revelatory gifts of tongues, prophecy and extraordinary knowledge have been withdrawn with the completion of the written word of God. Signs, wonders and miracles were given by God to authenticate the apostles' ministry and message. Since there are no more apostles, and the written word of God is complete, no man today has the ability to perform signs, wonders and miracles as he pleases. Tongues and prophecy were given *en masse* to the early converts in order to convince the Jewish believers that the gospel age had begun. These gifts were signs of "the last days" – in which Christ is proclaimed as the Saviour, and people from all nations are called out of the world to become members of His church.

The Cessationist position is based on the principle of the

sole authority of Scripture in all matters of doctrine and practice. It is not contradictory to the view that God can, and may, perform miracles in certain circumstances, in accordance to His will. The 1689 Baptist Confession of Faith states this truth as follows: "God, in His ordinary providence makes use of means, yet He is free to work without, above, and against them at His pleasure" (Chapter 5:3). God's power is seen more in His control over the myriad of everyday events than in a one-off miracle. The believer who keeps a close walk with his Lord will be no stranger to divine interventions and guidance, none of which needs to be miraculous. He will not trust in his feelings but in the word of God. He will seek to know the word of God and obey it. His whole life, including his feelings, will be regulated by the word of God.

This view of the revelatory and sign gifts, and of the Christian life, is opposed to that of the Charismatic movement. The Charismatic position is that the gifts have continued to today, or are being revived today. By claiming the revelatory gifts, the Charismatics are actually undermining the principle of the sole authority of Scripture. They are then open to all kinds of weird teaching, as has happened already. From the beginning of the Charismatic movement in the nineteen-sixties, claims of tongue-speaking and prophecy have been made. To these were added the casting out of demons, healings, and visions – none of which can be verified. Following these, there are the "holy laughter" and other antics – such as hissing like a snake and rolling on the ground – connected with the "Toronto Blessing". Where, and what, will all these lead to next? The Charismatics have no way of determining the direction of their faith. This is for the reason that they do not have a rule or standard to be guided by.

Why are the errors of the Charismatic movement so serious? Firstly, it has the effect of undermining the faith of true believers. While it is possible to have true faith in Christ without upholding the sole authority of Scripture, it is impossible to have a stable and clear faith without it. "Man shall not live by bread alone, but by every word that proceeds from the mouth of God" (Matthew 4:4). One's faith is sustained by the word of God. If the Bible is not the complete revelation of God, if it is not the sufficient and final word, the faith of the believer will have to depend on some other sources of authority.

Secondly, the errors of the Charismatic movement undermine the foundation of the Christian faith. The church is built on "the foundation of the apostles and prophets, Jesus Christ Himself being the chief cornerstone" (Ephesians 2:20). The church is being sanctified and cleansed "with the washing of water by the word" (Ephesians 5:26). When the foundation is undermined, the whole building will totter. While Christ will ensure that the gates of Hades do not prevail against His church (Matthew 16:18), it is required that His faithful followers "contend earnestly for the faith which was once for all delivered to the saints" (Jude 3).

Thirdly, the Charismatic movement brings great dishonour to the name of God. A distorted form of Christianity is being propagated as an expression of true Christianity. This is accompanied by a desire to fraternise with others who hold to a low view of Scripture, but who claim to have the gifts and related experiences. Their so-called tongue-speaking, prophecy and healings are done without biblical warrant. If someone were to carry out dubious activities in your name, or to forge your signature, you would feel terribly offended. The Charismatics are doing just that. They are carrying out their activities in the name of Christ. They are acting presumptuously. According to Old Testament teaching, they have to be stoned to death (Deuteronomy 18:20-22). According to New Testament teaching, church discipline needs to be applied upon them (2 Thessalonians 3:6, 14-15; Titus 1:10-11, 13).

It is our sincere hope that there will be those who are turned back from the errors of their ways. It is not good enough to claim that one is not an extreme Charismatic, or is a Non-charismatic who is sympathetic to the Charismatic position. Teachers of the word will be judged more strictly by God (James 3:1). Pastors will have to give an account of how they have taken care of the souls placed under their charge

(Hebrews 13:17). Christians have a duty to withdraw from those who are propagating errors in the name of Christ (Romans 16:17; 2 John 9-11).

The errors of the Charismatics need to be exposed. The correct teaching of God's word needs to be declared. The alarm needs to be sounded. Who will stand up for the truth in this age of apostasy?

Other books by the same author: